Praise for
Preaching the Headlines

"What does it mean to be Christian in a world where too often it seems like 'God is not'? For Lisa Thompson this is not an abstract question, but a practical one. And it is not a question reserved for theologians in the academy, but for preachers in the pulpit. In *Preaching the Headlines*, Thompson makes clear that being a Christian in the world ought to make a difference for the better, and it is a preacher's task to make that clear. For the preacher to do otherwise is to fail at their task of helping those to whom they preach live into what it means to be Christian. This book is a must-read for those who think preaching the gospel matters in a world where it too often seems like 'God is not.'"
—Kelly Brown Douglas, dean, Episcopal Divinity School, and Bill and Judith Moyers Chair in Theology at Union Theological Seminary

"In *Preaching the Headlines*, Lisa Thompson not only offers meaningful engagement with preaching, but extends an invitation to readers to think deeply about faith and life in the world. She calls each of us to courageous incarnate love practices through the process of communal questioning and reflection on significant social and ethical matters. If you want a bag of cheap homiletical tricks and tips, this is not the book for you. But if you desire to preach and embody what matters most in the world, this is God's gift to you. Open these pages and you'll discover prophetic and pastoral wisdom, with a faithfulness to the divine call to do justice, love kindness, and walk humbly with God."
—Luke A. Powery, dean, Duke University Chapel, and associate professor of homiletics at Duke Divinity School

"*Preaching the Headlines* is a powerful intervention for intra-Christian conversations on faith and justice, and it's also more than that. This book is a model for various communities, religious and otherwise, for how we can dig in collectively to the issues that matter most, with courage, commitment, and compassion."

—Simran Jeet Singh, senior fellow for the Sikh Coalition and columnist for Religion News Service

"*Preaching the Headlines* is a valuable conversation partner for those concerned with matters of faith and society. It calls for fewer divisions and greater fluidity in describing the relationship between Christian faith traditions and real-life issues on the ground. This relationship necessarily includes the acknowledgment of Christian culpability in injustice, as well as the true possibility of Christian transformation and constructive hope. The book foregrounds the responsibilities of Christian preaching traditions in co-creating a more just world. It also extends a way of thinking to anyone concerned with mobilizing Christian communities for meaningful participation in the world. This approach hinges on a nonnegotiable ethic of radical-love-practice that in its grit, uncertainty, and risks challenges us to say and do what matters most for our personal and collective well-being."

—Mark Labberton, president, Fuller Theological Seminary

PREACHING THE HEADLINES

PREACHING THE HEADLINES

Possibilities and Pitfalls

LISA L. THOMPSON

Fortress Press

Minneapolis

PREACHING THE HEADLINES
Possibilities and Pitfalls

31   30   29   28   27   26   2   3   4   5   6   7   8   9

Scripture quotations are from the New Revised Standard Version Bible © 1989
Division of Christian Education of the National Council of the Churches of
Christ in the United States of America. Used by permission.

Cover Design: Emily Harris Designs and Tory Herman

Print ISBN: 978-1-5064-5386-6
Ebook ISBN: 978-1-5064-5387-3

CONTENTS

CONTENTS

ACKNOWLEDGMENTS

I offer special thanks to and gratitude for the students who took this book in its course form during its developmental years. You continue to hold me accountable for thinking deeply and critically out of Christian faith traditions for their fullest and most hospitable possibilities for participating in a more just world. No amount of thanks will suffice for the colleagues, family, and friends who were conversation partners and readers while calling and demanding this project forward. This written project would not be possible without the support and funding of the Louisville Institute or the time to research and write granted by Union Theological Seminary in New York and Vanderbilt University Divinity School. We bring this offering for the good of the whole.

Introduction
We've Found Ourselves

Between my starting and finishing this project, we have found ourselves in the middle of the first global pandemic in over a century. COVID-19 brought us to our knees, placed us in our homes, limited our movements, changed the way we worked, and took away our very breath. The virus swept rural areas, small towns, cities, states, and countries. It left nearly no one and their daily lives untouched. Few people could claim invincibility, even as some were more apt to survive than others. Seismic shifts happened in our midst, and our lives changed drastically.

Communities of faith scurried to host virtual gatherings; they debated the legitimacy of worship via tele- and web conferencing. All the while, they asked questions about what to say and what to do in times like these. What to preach? How to preach? The grief, the anxiety, the ever-waiting joy, the immediate threat, the feelings of despair, and both our broken and working relationships were all palpable. All the things that make life *life* were apparent in different ways. Our conversations were infused with the stuff we experienced from day to day.

The pandemic literally suffocated the holy life force out of so many, and we were brought face-to-face with our ongoing imploding histories. We were jolted back to the reality of what it means to live in this world. Everything was cut away. The soul of our existence was exposed in both its shadows and its most luminous parts. Our deficits became more vivid as we were in search of a literal healing of the nations. We fought to do and name what was most important. We galvanized and rallied together in ways that showed our tenacity and our best aspects as humanity. Our worst aspects made us feel the depths of human splintering.

We were the dystopian future. Black and Brown people suffered more fatalities than those in other racial-ethnic groups. The deceased were put in body bags and stockpiled in refrigerated trucks. People without disposable income did the essential work required to sustain our access to basic necessities like groceries, transportation, and clean public spaces. They also were more readily exposed to illness, death, and irreparable financial loss. Incidents of domestic violence and addiction were invisible to some but more readily experienced by others; we were isolated for larger durations of time under psychological and financial stressors.

The flaws of the American experiment were laid bare. Corporations received stimulus monies that small businesses and individual households never received. Civilians and private corporations rushed to make masks and protective gear for health care workers who did not have supplies to care for the onslaught of patients. Food banks and unemployment lines were endless while supplies were depleted. Family and friends consolidated households. The US government deployed an unidentified national police force in unmarked vehicles on city streets and detained and battered civilians. These civilians were participating in public demonstrations despite the threat of the virus because of the ongoing disproportionate deaths of Black people at the hands of law enforcement. Armed and predominately white militias descended on government sites with and without protective facial masks to protest movement restrictions and the presidential election; they assembled in the absence of a national police force. Virus outbreaks happened as choirs convened for rehearsal, during stealth worship services, and as individuals packed indoor and outdoor spaces against public health advisements. The list goes on and on. These were only a fraction of the events that played out on the soil of the world's named superpower, the United States of America, during a presidential election year.

The pandemic that reshaped our lives in late 2019, throughout 2020, and into 2021 was a crisis, and it was a specific crisis with enduring effects. But such a crisis is not new, nor is enduring existential crises. Many have long known the battering of life in this world under an interconnected system that does not evenly distribute its force. They also have known we have the capacity to make the battering worse or participate in its alleviation. These realities existed before the pandemic, whether we were personally aware of them or not. But we were all forced to watch the dynamics and tensions unveil themselves in an acute way.

At least two things were made very clear. First, we cannot take bodily well-being for granted. Anything that threatens our physical well-being impacts our mental and spiritual well-being. A threat to one part of what it means to be human is a threat to all of what it means to be human and survive. Our fleshly viability matters. Second, we do not live in isolation, separated from a wider moving system that assumes shared—even if contested—agreements about how we live together in the world. This machine impacts health care, economics, food, shelter, safety, how we take leisure, laws and policies, and public and private assembly. And this machine does not work for everyone in the same way.

We found ourselves as the pandemic found us. We lived in different patterns. We lived with a different awareness of the world around us. And we actively tussled for what mattered most. Our survival was just as much local as it was national and global. Whatever happened across the ocean was no less important than what happened on the other side of our doors. Our personal well-being and responsibility were not separate from our collective accountability to one another.

For the first time, many Christian leaders and lay folk were asking, "In the context of our present world, what do we say and do out of our faith?" The world around us made it clear that our very existence is at risk.

Confronting Distinctions and Answers

Living amid and after a pandemic reality lessens the burden of this book. Fewer readers will need proof that what happens in the wider world impacts people of faith. Fewer need convincing that communities of faith are called to be critical and ethical participants in the world around us. This participation is not ad hoc but integral to who we are; it is integral to the flourishing of God's creation.

We, en masse, have been confronted. Life has called us on the false distinctions we've made between concepts like prophetic or pastoral, religious or secular, holy or unholy, worldly or godly, political or apolitical involvement. We are indicted by the outcomes of such distinctions. These distinctions led us to ask some questions for the first time. And they are the questions many never had the luxury to delay because they knew for themselves that survival was at stake and there were no distinctions between faith, personal survival, and collective accountability in the world at hand.

I also recognize that living amid and after a pandemic increases the burden of this book. Many will come to these pages looking for a how-to guide, a break-in-case-of-emergency book, or a codex of Scriptures and answers to the issues of the day for the sake of what they believe is preaching in relevant and meaningful ways. But multistep formulas will never give the preacher, the community, or the world what we most need for nimble proclamations and actions that attend to what matters most. We've always had those formulas, and we still have gotten to this very moment and the burning question, "How do we preach in times like these?"

As one who studies and teaches about preaching, an aspect of my work entails helping current and future faith leaders become more effective and responsible communicators of faith. Over the last decade, I have lived and taught in four very different cities—New York City, Pittsburgh, Chicago, and Nashville. I've worked and ministered in places ranging from a women's maximum-security prison to academic classrooms to houses of worship to virtual gathering spaces. I've thought about the ideas in this book with and taught them to students of Buddhist, Muslim, Jewish, Christian, Santerian, humanist, atheistic, and nonaffiliated backgrounds, and a myriad of changes happened in our world across that time and across those settings.

But the major questions and themes surrounding our points of tension and struggle have remained constant. The fundamental questions that arise in every class session, every syllabus, and every conversation with pastors, faith leaders, and others continue to be, What does it mean to be human? How do we live with integrity? How ought we interact with others, especially those who are different from us? And perhaps most importantly, How do we seek God's presence, guidance, and hopes in the midst of it all?

My approach to helping people formulate not answers but responses to these fundamental questions has also remained the same. The approach is one of curating knowledge, experience, and wisdom for the sake of resourcing the questions we are asking—namely, to help us ask better questions. To ask better questions, we need to expand our resources, frameworks of thinking, and conversation partners in order to determine which questions are most significant and critical.

Pursuing Better Questions and Responses

Better questions involve those that are more precise, help clarify, or render the most generative responses after we have asked them. These are not responses that close off possibilities and result in one answer (1 + 1 = 2) or that show you exactly how or what you must preach and say. Generative responses create possibilities, reveal different vantage points, and hold the potential to evolve as the world around us and life change. These responses push us continually into the process of envisaging a more just earth in real and relevant ways.

The path to better questions that attend to the times is twofold. It simultaneously seeks to understand the guiding values at work in the world around us and seeks to discern what living a life of faith involves in the ordinariness of our day-to-day lives.

Ordinariness does not mean uneventful; it means the actual things we ourselves and others experience on any given day. Our discerning the shape of public witness informed by faith happens alongside understanding what is actually taking place on the ground.

This pursuit of understanding includes exploring lived assumptions about what is most acceptable in our relationships with one another, how those assumptions look or play out in real time, and the impact these assumptions have on our ongoing lives together. Therefore, we inquire about what is both behind and beyond any singular event or media tagline. We consider histories and outcomes. As people of faith, we also consider why these are concerns based on what we claim we most value and hold true.

So what lies ahead is a framework for discernment and pragmatic decision-making. The framework assumes an awareness of our ethical responsibility as people of faith; it assumes that the scenarios will change but our obligations never do. The next go-around will not be a pandemic; it will be something else. Both today and tomorrow have their own challenges. There are no easy, certain, or error-proof routes in this work. Life is not static, so formulas will not do.

Saying What You Know

My primary intention or purpose is to help you better articulate what you know to be true. This applies no matter *how long* you've been attentive to matters of faith and society, be that two days or thirty years. My purpose or intention remains no matter *how* you've been attentive to matters of faith and society, be that through preaching, teaching, community organizing, blogging, thinking aloud with friends, advocacy, interfaith engagement, or public speaking. You know the world could be different and should be different. But why? You know people should not be treated as though they are dispensable. But why? In the depths of your being, you know something is off course. But why? And why should it matter to people of faith?

Preaching the Headlines extends a way of thinking about the world and faith. Again, this is *a* way, not *the* way. What you will find here are handles for us to grasp for analyzing and intuiting around real-life issues on the ground. Faith leaders are called to support a community's greatest needs while spurring the community's imagination for living in ways that participate with God in pulling forth a just creation. Christianity at times has both an unnamed and an overly pronounced influence on Western matters of faith and society, especially in the United States. Therefore, this work foregrounds the responsibilities of Christian preaching traditions in such contexts. For the preacher, this is a precursor to sermon development and design.

This way of thinking hinges on the assumption that a more just creation emerges as we reclaim the radicalness of love along with its grit, uncertainty, and risks. It calls upon a non-negotiable ethic within Christian traditions. A relationship with God is unequivocally connected to love. In fact, love practice demonstrates our continual awareness of God—love the Lord your God with all your heart, your soul, and your strength, and love your neighbor as yourself (Deut 6:4–5; Matt 12:37–40). Love practice is discipleship that moves based on awareness of God's future being at hand here and now and moving toward our neighbor. Radical love practice confronts the places where we are living most outside an awareness of God. These are the places where principalities and powers continue to devour all that is most innocent: life. Love is difficult and unscripted but also concrete. Love pushes through the grips of insidious hate for the sake of life.

I am most interested in being a conversation partner with those who, out of weariness but still with belief in better futures, want to conjure forth a different reality in our midst. This conjuring is not about secrets and fantastical measures untethered from the present reality. The work relies on building muscles of the heart, mind, soul, and body. Strengthening a muscle takes time, practice, tearing, and rebuilding. This conversation begins with sharpening our perceptions in order to determine how we show up in meaningful ways as engaged people of faith—no matter how subtle or rowdy the appearance.

Because the outcomes ahead of us are not fully scripted—beyond knowing we long for something more just, better, and closer to God's hopes—neither are the paths that get us closer to the other side. Preaching the headlines does not rely on biblical proof-texting or succinct road maps. While I include some explicitly practical components for preaching, this is not a text of tricks, tips, and techniques for preaching. This book does not label types of preaching as prophetic or pastoral, play within the lines of teaching and learning disciplines, or create divisions between profane and holy. The simple call here is for fewer divides and greater fluidity in our perceptions of the world around us and of our faith.

As we survey our world, we find ourselves. And we find ourselves finally trying to determine how to talk about and discern our way to what matters most.

1

Straight, No Chasers
Guiding Assumptions

Faith is not neutral. Preaching is a practice of faith. Neutrality in preaching is not attainable. These statements are flat-footed, I know, but this point of clarity is one of the most important to have moving forward. Often people contest attending to the social issues that impact our lives based on appeals to neutrality, not being political, or not wishing to offend. Such claims are contradictory in and of themselves. People of faith affirm values, name what seems most meaningful, and do so in the midst of ample alternative views. We take a position or have an opinion about whatever we most believe. Those opinions have implications, for better or worse, whether they are implied or explicit.

People often appeal to false neutrality when they cannot reconcile or find a reasonable bridge between faith and what they have heard. This irreconcilability brings us to one of the greatest pitfalls when attempting to lay bare all of life in speaking with people of faith. Preaching goes awry and misses the mark either by not naming what is at stake in the claims being made or by not naming why people of faith should be concerned based on the values they claim. Often leaders themselves do not know how to create better bridges between a tradition and what appears to matter most in the world. This inability may be due to a tradition that seems at odds with the concerns of life on the ground or that may perceive the world that emerges from Scripture and today's world as too far apart.

Without thoughtful, faith-informed insight, preaching that tries to engage the issues of the day risks becoming little more than a political stump speech, leaving many listeners to ask, "Was that a sermon?" But that to which we generally exclaim, "Yes! That's a sermon!" also may be in jeopardy. Unless a message candidly addresses life on the ground and moves to the collective concerns of life together, it succumbs to being an insular message hovering in the clouds. These messages never attend to faith as a dynamic and significant influence on the way we live and operate in the world.

One must be in conversation with the values that matter to people of faith when seeking their ethical and responsible involvement in what seems to matter most on the ground. Doing so with integrity goes beyond merely addressing political or social issues with general scriptural principles that distinguish right from wrong or proof-texting claims with Scripture. It calls for preachers to mine Scripture and tradition deeply and thoroughly in order to build relevant and meaningful bridges between Christian faith and life on the ground while remembering that faith itself is not bound to a text and tradition is not static. Faith is dynamic and takes on its lively textures in our lives in ways that supersede any texts, creeds, and doctrines—even as these things spur our ability to remember the stimulus for belief.

Guided Conversations

"Name as many faith words as you can. Call them out," she said. There were long pauses as the group struggled to answer, only mustering out a few words. "What stuff do you talk about at church?" she prodded. The momentum was slow going, but someone finally said, "Jesus!" Another person rang out, "Grace." Eventually, one person's response would spur someone else's response. By the end, we had filled two full-sized whiteboards with words: Hope. Communion. Discipleship. Revelation. Creation. God. Sex. War. Crucifixion. Food. Bodies. Joy. Peace. Love. Wrath. Judgment. Forgiveness. Prayer. Salvation. Repentance. Floods. Prophets. Atonement. And so on.

She then recounted a story from an immersion course she taught at the Mexico–US border. The details of the story are not as important as what came next. She asked each participant to survey their collection of words and to choose five, narrow that list to two, and then choose only one to use in a sentence about the story they had just heard. That sentence was each person's faith claim.

The instructions seemed simple enough: recall all that you know about faith, pay attention to this occurrence in the world, and now say something about it. The end goal was the same whether they started with something happening in the world or started with trying to recall what framed their thinking for understanding life with God and one another. The group had taken up this agonizing task in some form or another for seven weeks. There were no "right answers" to give. The process was about observation and responding. With a guide for the process, they thought and responded together, called upon what they knew, acquired new information, and tried collectively to discern their way to a more right-fitting response than the last.

I was exhausted from guiding countless sessions like this inside and outside the classroom. So I watched with relief as someone—who had done it longer than I—conducted this latest session: my former professor and now colleague, Viki Matson. Ten years had passed since I last sat in a classroom with Viki, watching her teach theological reflection by helping people do it on the spot. Now she was leading the sixth group of students over eight years to take my course Preaching the Headlines. This was the first time in all those years that a crossover was happening. One of my initial influencers in the creation of the course was guiding a group through the throes of its methods. The course was unfamiliar to Viki, but its methods were not. True, the process had morphed in the ten years that had passed as I used it alongside preaching methods and theories, but the essentials remained.

For years, I shrugged off comments from students like "Thank you" and "We couldn't have made it here without you." In those moments, through exhausting mind, heart, and spirit bending, the group had moved from piles of disjointed and vague thoughts to a coherent faith claim that rang with clarity and veracity as they surveyed what seemed to matter most in the times at hand. These were claims we believed had something or someone at stake on the other side of them. These were claims we felt people in our communities could understand, even in the presence of internal resistance. People may not have wanted to like the claims, as all their biases were challenged, for during the most generative sessions, even those of us in the room had to contend with our varying preferences and privileges. But folks would be hard pressed to deny them on the basis of their faith because the claims were formulated from the most bedrock values of Christianity.

After years of teaching, I needed my guide in the room that day more than I knew. Watching her reminded me that there was a method to this messy process. Some processes for thinking do more saliently open up the intersections between faith and life on the ground, including their pitfalls and possibilities. And those same processes breathe new air into long-used methods of sermon development and preaching—including how we encounter Scripture, how that encounter is impacted by our experiences, and how our faith claims buttress conviction and, ultimately, the message itself.

Eight years into teaching "my class," I still needed Viki and every single group of those students to hold up a mirror to my approach. They helped remind me of its hopes and sharpen its techniques for more right-fitting outcomes. More than I wanted them to, I realized the students' "Thank you" and "We couldn't have" statements over the years were saying the same about me as I had said about Viki in the room that day. The process and I were guides that were helping the students better articulate what they most believed to be true. But in earnest, we, collectively, were the guides we all needed.

Sitting back to assess the framework out of which we were working and thinking helped me return to the classroom and this project with a broadened yet clarified agenda. My sole agenda in the pages that follow is to offer preachers, people of faith, and those interested in communities of faith the same that Viki offered me, that I offered students, and, indeed, that students offered me in return. My hope is to offer a guided conversation about faith and life.

What It Is All About

By now, it should be discernible that *Headlines* in the title *Preaching the Headlines* is a metaphor for all those things our communities are struggling with and wondering about. The focus here is not on splattering sermons with headlines. In a literal sense, headlines are specific topics found in actual newspapers or in leading stories on television, radio, or online outlets, whether local or global. The greatest interest is in the stories behind and beyond the headlines and their interconnectedness across subject matters. These are the stories of the broader issues at play in the world. These issues impact our daily lives—both our flourishing and our demise. People of faith are trying to determine why and how these issues are of concern to them. Such clarification enables sustained responsiveness—whether that response is via a pulpit or not. The headlines are the times at hand. The headlines are our lives grounded in the present day.

✳ ✳ ✳

Preaching the Headlines assumes, crisis or not, that we communicate and live our faith as though our lives depend on it. This is not about life in a metaphorical sense, as if it was removed from the body; it's about life in its fleshy fullness—body, mind, and soul as one. The fullness of life includes its situated flourishing right here and right now. We're attending to life in its fragility and in its greatest possibilities. Life's greatest possibilities require the precursor of our survival. This is about real lives. Attending to life is not free of politics, but it is also not reduced to politics, party lines, allegiances, or divides.

This approach to preaching and conversation is about attending to the totality of life on the ground. Yes, we care for our spiritual, emotional, and physical needs in order for us to survive one more day in this dogged world. And yes, we attend to what makes the world so dogged in the first place. No border exists between pastoral care and the pursuit of justice, setting the world right-side up and calling out the chasm between the world as it is and could be. Both are concerns of God and both become concerns of those who claim to be people of God. This posture responds to the call of Micah 6:8 to do justice, love kindness, and move forward humbly with God.

Practically speaking, the preacher remains aware that in their midst is a survivor of domestic violence along with an abuser or someone who cannot make ends meet as well as someone who can help others meet their ends. The preacher remains privy to the person with limited mobility or hearing loss. The preacher is clear there are those with skin hues, family lineages, and life partnerships different from their own. As life goes, people have lost loved ones, and they themselves may be terminally ill. So the preacher chooses their language and body gestures and interprets Scripture in ways that take seriously what total well-being and life abundant mean amid all these realities. In other words, the preacher is accountable to each life before them. Most importantly, the preacher and community engage more right-fitting resources for this work—whether those resources are inside or outside the faith tradition.

Leaders think and communicate to sustain life, which means they are committed to greater humility and risk-taking. The preacher does not give answers because they do not have all the answers. Instead, they extend an invitation. The invitation is one that creates a different paradigm for how we think and act—to become more engaged persons, no matter how big or small the corners of the world we occupy. This invitation is made possible by faith leaders themselves asking better and more critical questions without knowing where the responses may lead.[1] The push is for people of faith to claim their agency to think critically about, imagine, and pursue lifesaving transformations of the world at hand.[2] Salvation becomes just as tangible as it is spiritual.

The greatest implications here are for supporting accountable and engaged people of faith. All of this assumes people of faith do not depend solely on answers from religious leaders and that they learn to pursue their own questions and hunches. Their dependence on religious leaders is one that holds leaders accountable for opening a space for exploration. In this space, they may judge for themselves *together* and access their capacity to think and act.[3] These are matters of relationship, agency, self-leadership, and communal volition. This agency may take a variety of forms, including organizing communities, bringing affordable healthy food options to towns and eliminating "food swamps,"[4] supporting local businesses, caring for people in nursing homes, helping formerly incarcerated people make a successful transition from prison, working to dismantle the prison industrial complex itself, being mindful of ableism in worship services, advocating for public policies that are just and compassionate, showing up at the protest line and local city council meetings, and more. There's plenty of need to go around. The ability to engage the world around us in more responsible ways requires our willingness to think and interrogate in community.

Claims of Clarity and Substance

This orientation to the life of faith is not about relative truths or nonsubstantive claims. Instead, the community gains greater clarity about what it holds most true about its traditions and the possibilities that lie therein and beyond. For starters, we become clear that we cannot compromise our neighbor in the name of loving God. Loving God is not a warm, fuzzy, commercialized emotion; it is about living mindful of God. To live in awareness of God requires uncompromising effort in living mindful of our neighbor. The mandates of love, given in both the Old and the New Testaments of Christian Scriptures (Deut 6:4–5; Matt 12:28–33), demand the entire self; a half-hearted effort won't do. We are to orient the very seat of our beings—our hearts, our minds, and our might—in the direction of God and neighbor. This mandate is not "works righteousness" but a "turning toward" that leads to "doing."

This turning toward our neighbor does not erase or diminish our own well-being. In fact, how we attend to our neighbor reflects the health of our disposition toward ourselves—"love your neighbor as yourself" (Mark 12:31). Thinking less worthily of ourselves is not the way of loving our neighbor. We are not called to suffer to the point of our own deterioration and demise in the name of someone else. But practicing hate toward our neighbor also diminishes our own humanity. Practicing hate toward our neighbor illuminates the self-hate present in the need to claim ourselves as better or more worthy of the fullness of life than another. Ultimately, practicing love toward our neighbor reflects the vibrancy of our self-awareness and our awareness of God.

Neither the community of faith nor preaching holds claim to less, but both hold claim to more. They err on the side of love of God and love of neighbor in their most vibrant, radical, and embodied forms. They hold claim to life's viability and love having the final authority over whatever we say and do in the name of faith. They claim our state of relationships as a flicker of the transforming realm of God[5] that we hope is to come, a realm that breaks in from time to time, as it is simultaneously already here but not yet.

The assumption here is not only that the enduring structures of power and dominance that create the greatest woes in our midst will "be toppled," but that we, as people of faith, have "personal agency in God's vision" for that toppling and a more just world.[6] Evelyn Parker describes this working relationship between hope and agency as *emancipatory hope*.[7] We are invited to participate in both the toppling over and the realm to come. So in the face of many unknown "answers" to the question of how to love God, ongoing valid responses consider what love of neighbor requires of us in any given moment. Somehow our willingness to pursue more just relationships here and now affirms our awareness of God. Love of God and neighbor is the emancipatory hope we practice for the fullness of life. The order is tall, but collectively we move toward fulfilling it.

Life and Tradition

Our claim of loving God and neighbor may lead to reassessing, expanding, or even recanting previous claims or traditions. This claim of love requires more openness and humility in our future claims. As we assess life on the ground, we may recognize that some things we hold dear may not remain viable if we truly privilege sustaining life and radical love practice toward neighbor. This means *every* neighbor regardless of religious affiliation, social status, or place in the world.

If our previous or future claims are used to perpetuate insidious hate, then those claims fail under the authority of life-sustaining radical love practices. And so we must continually revisit such claims to reassess and clarify. Reassessing does not mean having tidy answers beforehand; it means we are clear that any claim that opposes life and love of neighbor is regarded with some suspicion.

This means we reassess the ways we've interpreted Scriptures and the tradition because life being at risk gives enough cause for an openness to interrogation. When children's lives are not preserved and protected, we reassess what we've claimed about them before God and people. We reassess how we interpret Scriptures and the traditions regarding the full humanity of children. Similarly, we reassess our claims about the relationship of humans to creation if bioweapons are increasingly used and the natural world continues to deteriorate and heads toward destruction.

If sustaining all creation and responding out of a commitment to a radical love practice matter most to God, then this is what matters most to the community of faith. It may challenge us to refrain from holding on to traditions, rituals, and values that once were a part of our journey but will not sustain our futures as communities of faith. Clarity about what matters most helps the tradition of faith remain viable into its future; the alternative is succumbing to the death of irrelevance by dwelling on what matters least of all.

Life and Scripture[8]

Expanding our approaches to Scripture and its interpretation is one of the greatest challenges associated with preaching the headlines. Having an ongoing disposition toward any given text is different from making erroneous connections between multiple passages of Scripture and a topic of the day—biblical proof-texting. Here, interpreting for preaching becomes multifocal, requiring attention to a nimble movement between texts, their historical contexts, the community at hand, and the wider world. The most effective preaching recognizes that we are best able to tell the story of biblical texts anew when we listen deeply to them as the stories of a world that is different from ours yet familiar in that the people long ago lived with enigmas, power struggles, vulnerabilities, pursuits of life, failures, and successes similar to our own.

We honor the understanding that while the history of a text and its context are important, they never supersede contemporary contexts. Final interpretations take shape in the lives of those who will receive them. We are accountable to the lives in front of us at any given moment and to sustaining them instead of hindering them. Some texts make our accountability to these lives more concrete than other texts, but that accountability is always present. What we make of a person cut into pieces and strewn across the land in Judges 19 is no less significant than what we make of accounts of the crucifixion of Jesus in the Gospels when it comes to the lives before us.

Therefore, we interpret Scripture in conversation with others, not in the silos of private studies.[9] We do so in order to remain accountable to real life on the ground. Decisions are guided by humility and charity, recognizing our historical inclinations to read Scripture in ways that align with power.[10] We ask questions of texts, interrogate them, and observe their depictions of people stumbling, their outright failure, or them getting closer to all that it means to love God and neighbor. We recognize and do not dismiss the story of human fallibility that bleeds from its pages, even in the name of God.

Scripture cannot be dismissed when trying to move people of faith to more engaged action in the world. No matter how unsatisfactory and incomplete the question "What does the Bible say?"

is, we still must attend to it in some way or another. I've witnessed people reject messages wholesale due to an absence of any sustained or adequate attention to Scripture. Jettisoning Scripture jettisons listeners. There exists a temptation to avoid Scriptures that are troublesome or violent or that leave us baffled. The alternative is to lean into these texts and explore them deeper and with more integrity in front of the community. Raise the questions about these texts that lie dormant within all of us.[11] This is what it means to pursue responses instead of answers.

Approaching interpretation in this way does not diminish the role of Scripture; instead, it recognizes its role in the lives of listeners and relies on it. We work with Scripture's recognized authority to do something more life sustaining than we have done in the past. Knowing that Scripture is touchable, invites our questions, and relies on our observations is what retains its ongoing sacred nature as a living and relevant document.

Doing Faith Talk Better

Attending to the fullness of life on the ground and its sustenance requires doing better faith talk. Doing better faith talk means being confrontational in the best ways possible. We must confront our use of core strands of Christian tradition to perpetuate injustices. We can readily see in history how easy it is to influence social order by coating it with a Christian veneer. This dynamic is at work in assumptions about gender and ethnic-racial superiority. This dynamic is present in slavery and human trafficking in ancient and more contemporary times. This dynamic hovers around everything from the Crusades to genocides to the denial of rights to people seeking general physical safety and equal pay. In short, one spin on the story of faith further exacerbates the violence and tensions in our world, while a different spin on the story of faith creates more generative and life-giving outcomes.

We seek to do faith talk better in order to better translate the matters of the day for people of faith. The how of preaching the headlines comes through revisiting the story of faith, which recognizes its sacred nature for people of faith. Put another way, the work before us is that of doing sacred storytelling differently.[12]

People of diverse Christian faith traditions are united by a sacred story. Over time, we have discerned this story in conversation with Scripture in our worshipping communities. This story often begins with God's offer to be in relationship with creation and continues with our living into that relationship. Along the way, we also see how hindrances keep that relationship from being fully realized, and that grace helps us sustain that relationship. Admittedly, a lot of life happens between the books of Genesis and Revelation. There are betrayals, births, deaths, wars, wedding banquets, a crucifixion and resurrection, the earth opening up in judgment to swallow a creation gone astray, and the promises of a new heaven and a new earth.

This is a vibrant story. And different communities accentuate different parts of the story. But ask people who are part of Christian traditions what they believe, and no matter how shallow or complex their responses may seem, it will inevitably connect with some aspect of the aforementioned story. We mark our liturgical calendars, sing hymns, and create worship services around this story: Advent, Christmas, Epiphany, Lent, Holy Week (including Good Friday), Easter, and Pentecost.

In attending to the fullness of life on the ground, this sacred story is a reference point for addressing questions related to our life with God, our relationships with others, and our efforts to pursue a just world. As stated earlier, these questions have at their core a key assumption that the greatest mandates before us are "Love God with all our being" and "Love our neighbor as ourselves." These commandments connect any given strand of the Christian tradition to the next. And this connection holds no matter how different one tradition might seem from another and no matter how different one tradition might "color in" the details of the sacred story. The work of the preacher is to determine how to color in the details in a way so that listeners can discern the familiar story but experience it and its connection anew to the times at hand.

Doing faith talk better reclaims the story of faith from its most dangerous possibilities while filling out its details for alternative ones. The task is not to simply reiterate the story or even offer an alternative one. The task is to tell of other possibilities in a way that resonates just as profoundly as the story a community already knows. We find our way to other possibilities by posing the question, *What if there is a different way to tell the story of faith?*

For different outcomes in our world, we need to pursue alternative possibilities within the story of faith. And this begins with being clearer about what exactly we do and do not intend when discussing a narrative that carries meanings that are often taken for granted. At the core of reclaiming and filling out the story of faith, the preacher and community ask, "What if it is *not this but that?*" or "What if it is not *only* this but also that?" They interrogate every assumption made about the story of faith and how it is told:

"What if _____ is *not this but that?*" or "What if _____ is *not only this* but also that?"
    sin
    grace

reconciliation
redemption
salvation
discipleship
And if so, what does it yield or make possible in the world today?

And finally, what is required to help move this from possibility to reality?

The key here is offering more possibilities for what a relationship with God and neighbor might entail while looking to our collective well-being without limiting the tradition to personal sins and their regulations.

These what-if questions make way for a process of imaginative brainstorming for concrete possibilities. By "imaginative brainstorming," I do not mean a process that lacks substance or significance. Instead, the process relies on a disposition of openness while harnessing all one knows in order to perceive other possibilities in both the world and the tradition.[13] Such exercises of the imagination have moral dimensions and possess clarity about what is at stake in the world at hand. It is a form of possibility thinking[14] done in hopes of discerning the ways in which the world at hand aligns or misaligns with hopes of a just earth and God's kin-dom come. This imaginative brainstorming leads to commitments as well as being and doing differently in the world around us.[15]

The obligation of Christian communities of faith is to consider what is at stake in what we proclaim and how to discern with integrity. For this to happen, we remain aware of interactions between the world, sacred texts, and the faith tradition. And we seek to interpret them all in ways that do not perpetuate additional harm in our midst but rather contribute to better sustaining a just creation. This isn't about being a do-gooder or acquiescing to the values of the social order of the day. This is about erring on the side of love of God and love of neighbor in their most vibrant and lived forms. Our final decisions grow from understanding more fully what we have long called discipleship, or following the way.

What Lies Ahead

The easiest way to describe what lies ahead and its shape is to return to one of the earliest instructions in this chapter: recall all that you know about faith, pay attention to this thing in the world, and now say something about it. In the following chapters, I dig a bit deeper into select things happening in our world, their core tensions, and the risks present if these things continue. I then think aloud about faith talk and its possibilities in attending to those things. And finally, I choose *one* aspect of Christian traditions that might help us talk about those chosen topics with God's just creation in mind. You may choose others, and I hope you do. I chose these topics to demonstrate a process, not as an exhaustive list of concerns.

The chapters include enduring questions we may bring to Scripture or the world around us for ongoing engagement with any of these topics. Each of these chapters ends in the same place that our conversations and observations will end in real life: with the humble recognition that as we gain greater clarity about what we know and how we know it, we gain greater clarity about what we don't know and what we need to learn more about. At some point, we recognize that the tradition of faith must be in conversation with the expansive gifts of knowledge that surround us.

The final chapter of the book includes three "in-practice" segments to accompany chapters 2, 3, and 4. These segments distill very practical previews of how the core matters discussed and their reframing may and should cause additional questions to arise when engaging the particulars of any passage of Scripture (or scenario in the world at hand). Each of these segments includes excerpts from my own sermons, only to demonstrate a possible outcome for preaching when using these frameworks of thinking.

As I made decisions about whether or not to include this final section, I literally felt the enduring echoes of practitioners saying, "I cannot take this back to my people!" These segments are my enduring encouragement and retort, "Yes, you can!" These segments are also a public test of my accountability to those practitioners and the masses who need material that can be translated to accessible outcomes. Accessible outcomes rely on building bridges based on the world people know and what they believe already, even if it means using those very same bridges to expand what they believe and know.

What lies ahead is one way of thinking about life in conversation with faith for the sake of a more just world. That just world, even our limited imaginings of it, hinges on a willingness to think more deeply about what it means to forego the "safe" route in favor of a more responsible route, one that treats the people before us with care as our collaborative partners.[16] This is for the person who proclaims a message week in and week out, once a month, or once in a proverbial blue moon, with or without a pulpit, in everyday life. This is for the community who believes or wants to believe in calculated risk taking.

2

Fleshy Parts
Race, Gender, Sex, Abilities, and Other Bodily Matters

And the Word became flesh and lived among us.
—John 1:14

We're beginning with what I'm calling the "fleshy parts" because of the prominence of our bodies in our daily interactions, our experiences, and the tensions that arise in our midst. These fleshy parts of life involve our bodies. We know the world based on how we experience it. We navigate the world in our bodies, collecting and sharing experiences along the way. We sort and sift these experiences, information, and emotions through our bodies.

Fleshy parts of life pertain to our skin and its hues, our mental and physical abilities, and who we do and do not have sexual and nonsexual partnerships with. They also extend to our perceived vitality or wisdom due to age, our treatment of and the characteristics we assign to gender, how we associate value and self-worth with how much a person weighs or the amount of physical space they take up, and a host of other things. Every day we experience the burdens and joys of being *living*, or spirit-filled, *flesh*.[1]

Our experiences are squarely connected to what it means to live in a human body. How our bodies are interpreted by society and faith traditions greatly impacts those experiences. This includes what we should and should not do, where we do and do not belong, and who exactly gets to say so. Matters of the flesh and their impact on our interactions are connected to people's ability or inability to flourish here and now. Without question, the choices we make in attending to matters of the flesh impact someone's physical livelihood.

The preacher is attuned to these choices when helping a community assess what love of God and love of neighbor look like today. The preacher privileges two agendas in this work. First, the community must discern what our world currently communicates about the worth of every person and who is most vulnerable due to these perceptions. Second, the community enters a conversation with the faith tradition in a way that foregrounds our created integrity—bodies sustained by the holy life force enshrouded in flesh. These commitments create a space for the community to consider what they might say and do to create a way of life that is abundant for all flesh.

Behind and beyond the Headlines

Concrete matters of the flesh are behind and beyond the headlines, as are tensions around these matters as well as the risks involved if the status quo continues. As our flesh is subject to interpretation, human worth is subject to interpretation. The demise of human life is a viable option if we do not consciously engage matters of the flesh in preaching.

Tangible Matters

We witness the multiple ways we interpret something or someone simply taking up space in the world. For instance, the headline "Husband Kills Three Daughters after Unsuccessful Restraining Order to Stay Away from Estranged Wife and Children" gives us immediate descriptors of the persons involved.[2] The description presumably includes three girls, a woman, and a man in a familial relationship. It also details the need for a restraining order, from which we may conclude the situation involves a history of threat, harm, or violence. And finally, the violent death of three young girls is the described outcome.

Who was involved in the account of this headline is just as significant as the event that occurred. The headline is connected to a long history of domestic violence and its intersection with gendered violence, violence against children, and the continual lack of safety and protection for both women and children. That lack of safety and protection is further complicated by ineffective legal avenues for seeking protection—"restraining order." The people involved in the incident are significant in any encounter we have, as a history accompanies those people in that very interaction.

This headline points to the way we perceive the value of women and children and their lives. It declares something of how others perceive the right of women and children to flourish without the threat of premature death. These are matters of the flesh because they are issues that impact physical bodies and their ability to live or die. These also are matters of the flesh because of the way women and children are sometimes treated due to their physicality and the way they take up space.

The tensions we experience around our physical bodies take on exponential qualities with every additional layer of social location that makes us distinct in the world. For example, a layer of inequity may be added to a person based on their gender and age when we place the aforementioned headline alongside something like the following one: "#BringBackOurGirls—276 Chibok Schoolgirls Kidnapped."[3]

In April 2014, 276 Nigerian schoolgirls were kidnapped by the militant organization Boko Haram. For a span of three and a half years, the girls were unrecovered, with little media attention given to their kidnappings. In April 2021, seven years later, 112 of the schoolgirls remain missing. This was the story not of one girl but of nearly three hundred girls from a country in the continent of Africa. The media's lack of pushing this story to the forefront of the news was criticized as a continuation of the perpetual disregard for the lives of Black women and girls in general and African women and girls specifically.

The situation of the Chibok schoolgirls revealed many layers—the layers of race and ethnicity and the layer of violence based on gender and age. The case raises concerns for ensuring the safety of the most vulnerable and their access to resources, financial and otherwise, in the complex landscape of national and global politics. Life on the ground contends with a hierarchy, of which flesh counts the most.

How we treat someone and dictate their fate is an extension of how we perceive their autonomy and right to live without threat and oversight. Ultimately, we act on those perceptions. These are sentiments that impact someone's ability to make choices about the fate of their own physical bodies. These choices include what they do or don't do with their body, how their voice is respected or silenced in such choices, and their right to protection from the myriad of hate's destructive forces. Our process of making daily decisions about human worth and dignity as they intersect with embodiment lies at the core of these headlines and many more. These concrete matters of the flesh are further complicated by the matters related to age, physical and cognitive abilities, sexuality, mental and physical health and wellness, race, gender, and more.

These matters of the flesh address issues of living full lives and the threats of premature death. Movements such as Black Lives Matter,[4] #MeToo,[5] and #SayHerName;[6] LGBTQI+ advocacy; reproductive policies; voting rights acts; and all manner of civil rights actions also attend to these matters of the flesh. Each of these matters connects to our bodies and how we make determinations about our personal autonomy, collective fate, and ability to live.

Tangible Tensions

We live in a world where we inequitably interpret human worth, which has long led to the existing tensions related to how we both perceive and treat each other as beings of spirit and flesh.[7] We have assigned more value to some people over and against others. Our inequitable assessments of human worth are often broken down along the lines of those matters associated with the fleshy parts of our lives, whether or not we readily acknowledge those breakdowns. Divisions and disproportionate power in our relationships exist along those same lines.

Inequitable systems and unjust assessments of people flow from drawing unilateral equivalences between distinctives, diversities, and deficiencies. Our conflation of distinctiveness and deficiency leads to our seeing some people as less valuable than others. When we do this, we diminish their humanity and thus the sanctity of their lives. But thinking differently of others is not where the road stops.

Our patterns of thinking make way for abuses against the sanctity of human life. These abuses are the violence we witness in our midst as we declare the right to own the fate of our neighbor. This violence includes those things that wound spirit or flesh, creating suffering and ongoing fractures in our relationships with one another. Over time, we have consistently assigned some people a more inferior status than others, thus diminishing the perceived humanity of those groups of people over time.

The many *-isms* and other debasing phobias we have come to know and name are the result of our patterns in assigning an inferior status to people. This looks like disproportionate threats to the livelihoods of folks who identify as children, women, queer, Black, Brown, Indigenous, disabled, elderly, and so much more. These *-isms* and other debasing phobias include things such as racism, colorism, sexism, queerphobia, heterosexism, fatphobia, ableism, and ageism. No list can contain it all because this is about a way of living.[8] Divisions in our relationships to one another are represented by these *-isms*. These *-isms* are only one inefficient way of attempting to describe how we are impacted by the social realities of the world around us.[9] These divisions and hierarchies within actual living flesh impact people and their access to resources and safety as well as the ordering of our public and private lives together. These are matters not of identity politics but of our very beings—the core of who we are—and having a viable chance at living.

Tangible Risks

The ways we do or do not assess human worth create undue suffering. We have witnessed the most insidious version of this suffering:

people groups being killed off through genocide or being incrementally brutalized over time. This undue suffering cuts people off from the ability to flourish and contributes to ongoing premature deaths. These threats to flourishing play out in what seem to be innocent or nonconsequential forms, such as words and sentiments about people. Threats to flourishing also take shape as outright violations to physical bodies.

Prolonged suffering and premature death remain at stake if we continue down these paths. When we assess someone to be of inferior worth than another, we create an environment in which it is permissible to dominate and subdue others based on these very assessments. Our practices of domination and subduing are varied, but they are connected by the ongoing ways they make it permissible to put lives at risk.

The alternative path of love requires honoring life and confronting the ways we disregard human life. The preacher takes a risk by preaching about matters of the flesh. Such preaching may be prone to meeting resistance. Some people are simply uncomfortable talking about some of the issues. Others mark their progression in the world by centering domination and placing others in an inferior status to themselves. Giving up the privileges of the dominant place in relationships can be a larger hurdle to confront. But greater risks are involved if this exploration is not undertaken.

We cannot gloss over any of these issues as we assess what we believe to be true about created integrity as a God-given entity. What we say to be most true about matters of the flesh has concrete outcomes and impacts our ability to practice love of God and love of neighbor. The preacher's task is to expose the ways we diminish others in the flesh because of who they are as physical beings; it is an exposure of our conflations of distinct and deficient. The work of the preacher is to expose such unilateral equivalences when they appear both in the sacred texts of the tradition and in the everyday life of the world.

Exploring Faith

When attending to matters that pertain to and impact our physical lives and bodies, the preacher seeks ways to illuminate diversities in our midst to ensure such diversity is not seen as being in some way deficient or lacking as the creation of God. And even more bluntly, physical bodies and the matters connected to those bodies are not inherently *sinful*. Matters of the flesh are not to be feared or vilified, whether they pertain to race, sex, sexuality, gender, abilities, or otherwise. Matters of the flesh are not to be used to inflict suffering.

Many will say, "Obviously!" However, we have proven over time that we do not honor the diversity of ways in which we physically show up in the world. Our declaration that no one should be treated as less than another has amounted in some instances to language not worth its salt in terms of substantively impacting our actions. The times call for communities of faith to explore the furthest implications of what it means to be created with inherent integrity. The times call for exploring the implications of anything that stops short of the full affirmation of each person. The times call us to attend to our violations of the human body as the presence of evil and a participation in hate that turns us away from relationship with God.[10]

Tangible Changes

Remaining accountable to matters of the flesh in ways that support the flourishing of human life requires recovering and prioritizing human life. We must recover human life as a fully integrated experience of our being flesh and spirit. This recovery needs to happen in Scripture and in the world. Furthermore, we must acknowledge how we treat people as a reflection of what we perceive to be most true about the fullness of their humanity, their worth, and humaness—no exceptions. The goal is to align action with belief. The possibilities of transformative actions reside in the community understanding the tangible risks of doing nothing and imagining what substantive changes in our relationships would entail.

For change to happen, the community cannot espouse false equivalences in ways that allow taking consolation in a commitment to "treat people nice" while retaining inequity at the core of our beliefs. Such commitments are surface level and will not result in long-term transformative action. We need to go beyond platitudes such as "Hate the sin, love the sinner" or "Women were created for different purposes than men but are not to be mistreated." Time has shown us such surface commitments justify the domination of our neighbor. The contradictions within them do not result in significant changes that move us closer to more just visions of living together.

The preacher seeks to push open enough space for earnest communal interrogation. We interrogate if and why we find it possible to read "any flesh" as sinful or inferior as the creation of God. Put a different way, the community enters a process of discerning if and why they perceive some forms of embodiment as God created and good and others as deviant and worthy of suffering. The focus needs to be on who suffers most from these perceptions. True discernment will either exasperate or alleviate the tensions in our midst. The old adage "The proof is in the pudding" shapes the process. The results of our exposed beliefs are what we're held accountable for.

The pitfalls caused by the dueling flesh and spirit dynamics within Christian faith traditions complicate the tensions with which we already live. The community searches for outcomes that do not vilify the body in honor of the spirit by declaring flesh as insignificant or bad and the spirit as good.[11] To this end, the community confronts the least helpful portions of its own tradition.

Confronting ongoing threats to the flourishing of human life hinges on a deep inquiry into our beliefs about physical bodies. This type of inquiry moves beyond establishing rules and orders and a list of dos and don'ts, such as do have sex, don't have sex; have sex with this person, not that person; obey and don't be disobedient because it's the will of God; be seen and not heard; or race matters, and we don't see color. This type of inquiry requires asking the question, What do we believe about what it means to live as beings of spirit and flesh?

Tangible Faith Talk

Our commitment to honoring the totality of what it means to be the created of God, flesh and spirit, requires discerning ways of living accountable to those beliefs. Living in more accountable ways emerges from listening deeply to the experiences of people who suffer in the name of all that is connected to their flesh. Those experiences of suffering reveal how the created of God are being dishonored. As we attend to these experiences in our midst, people are offered the ability to name for themselves what flourishing does *not* look like as the community gathers around to imagine what flourishing might entail. At minimum, survival hinges on not doing further harm and paying close attention to living, breathing flesh.

Christianity is fleshy at its core. The tradition has a precedent for acknowledging what it means to live in a physical body in this world and God's own incarnational identification with that experience. This precedent is the avenue for change. The incarnational, in-the-flesh foundations of Christianity are gateways for thinking about faith and ethical frameworks regarding matters of life and our physical bodies alongside God's hopes.

God creating beings of flesh, coming to us in the flesh of Jesus Christ, and dwelling among flesh in relationship is the core of the Christian faith story. This story carries forward the plot of the Gospels. Jesus identifies with the physical human experience, suffers it, and physically takes on the wounds and trauma of that experience in crucifixion. Postresurrection Jesus appears in a physical body and then invites the disciples to touch his flesh and its wounds as he asks for food and something to drink. His resurrection does not deny the presence of a body nor its wounds but carries them.

Shelly Rambo suggests that we witness a more "porous" relationship between life at hand and a fate to come in the resurrection of Jesus.[12] She argues that the resurrection reveals *"life resurrecting amid the ongoingness of death."* Jesus encounters those who both knew and did not know him, sits in community with the disciples, and invites them to probe his wounds.[13] The resurrection signifies a "transfiguring of life," not a negation or erasure of it or that of the wounds.[14] While Rambo specifically addresses the wounds of trauma and processes of healing, the role and place of the physical body of Jesus are helpful when we consider why and how we attend to matters of the flesh in preaching.

The fleshy ministry of Jesus culminates with the resurrection. The hope of resurrection has a presence and is tangible in form. This hope is not simply one of future possibilities; it is grounded in experiencing the transformation of life in the moment right before us. We live in the shadow of death, which is ongoing and lingers near. The resurrection does not ignore the realities of suffering or the "ongoingness of death"[15] but in some ways calls us to examine and probe the marks of death in our midst. These marks are ever present in our beings and bodies as living flesh. We don't ignore our carnal reality but rather embrace it in the sure hope of the resurrection of both body and spirit.

Tangible Possibilities for Preaching

An incarnational faith does not leave room to ignore sufferings that are carnal at their core. Instead, it reclaims what happens to our physical bodies as being connected to our vitality and flourishing. The preacher points to the transfiguring possibilities that the resurrection bears witness to in real—and not abstract—ways. The community confronts the unholy judgments we make about human worth, which cause undue suffering. In contrast, the community is called to enact the grace and hope of the resurrection, which perpetuates ongoing life. Possibilities for life emerge from interpreting texts, the story of faith, and our world when we consider matters of the flesh, the status quo, and confronting these issues in our daily lives.

First, the preacher interprets both Scripture and the world at hand to recover people, their lives, and their suffering from insignificance and invisibility. As the preacher does this work, the folks of the scriptural text are encountered as living, breathing, and moving flesh, and their lives become just as real as the lives around us. In the same way, today's headlines, conversations, and ideas are not abstract but connected to actual flesh-and-blood neighbors. Therefore, the preacher works to *humanize* whenever and wherever possible. Again, this work recovers what is present already.

Throughout Scripture, we read stories of the Holy One encountering people and interacting with their physicality and needs. Just as despair and death encroached upon Hagar and Ishmael in the wilderness, they are provided a source of water after God discloses its location. Many stories of Jesus entail miracles and him healing the physical bodies of people, a reversal of their places of suffering, and their reorientation to the wider community. Jesus frees the one labeled the demoniac who had been cast away to the cliffs and chained because of his mental state. Jesus brings physical healing to the woman whose hemorrhaging caused her isolation from the community. Jesus does not hurry up and skip over their bodies and the residual impact in their lives for the sake of a bigger message alone.

Second, the preacher's agenda is to address inequitable interpretations of human worth and created integrity in this work of recovery. This primarily means pushing against the grain of the status quo wherever it is found in the world, in the text, or in the faith tradition. They go this route because the gospel demands it and because of the alternative possibilities of a relationship with one another—and the embodied grace that helps get us closer to those possibilities—are life sustaining. In earnest, the preacher seeks to reclaim our created integrity at every turn. Life and its ability to be sustained have authority over any given outcome.

Third, the preacher interprets the tradition of faith and the world with an awareness of systemic *and* personal issues at all times, without letting one outpace the other. While approaching the work, the preacher keeps the widest consideration of people in mind, their viability, and their access to participating in the hopes of God. For instance, whatever decisions we make about the presence and value of people in Scripture, whether implicitly or explicitly, we are making some corollary judgments about the worth and the full humanity of people in our world. The same holds true about the judgments one makes about the values at play within the larger world of the text.

To this end, the preacher has to discern how to lift up the personal consequences people suffer and the social issues that contribute to that suffering. One of the pitfalls when moving this way in preaching is the challenge of attending to the *-isms* mentioned earlier as systematic and structural evils alone. They are indeed systematic and structural evils, *and* they land upon physical bodies and create specific untenable conditions in the lives of people. Recovering the personal means recovering the emotions, senses, and all that makes us human—including all the joys and sorrows. Even systemic prejudice or evil is fleshy at its core. The human experience is the perpetual gateway for showing our corporate culpability.

Finally, the preacher becomes accountable to the mechanics of a sermon that contribute to or alleviate undue suffering in our midst. This includes choices of language, images, illustrative material, and final sermon outcomes. Greater attention is given to those things that rely on the very *-isms* the community seeks to address. Consideration must be given to what physical abilities are being assumed (i.e., hearing, mobility, cognitive, and more). Further consideration is given to how gendered stereotypes are foregrounded and the ways violence is implicitly or explicitly condoned. Preachers attend to ethnic and racial distinctions, including anti-Jewish sentiments and their role in Christian preaching; they attend to the often associations between black and darkness with evil and negativity alongside the associations of white with good and positivity. Attention is paid to anything that may diminish the humanity of another. Every choice counts.

Therefore, the work of the preacher is to ask questions that help *flesh out* the people and histories present in the text and world today while being clear that what they ultimately decide to say can build or dissolve bridges to better futures. The following are enduring questions that we bring to Scripture and the world when attending to matters of the flesh and preaching. Of most importance is asking these questions in a process of brainstorming and free association without first trying to determine if the response is right or wrong:

* Get in touch with the bodily experience. What feelings, sounds, sights, smells, vibrations, colors, or images come to mind as we encounter this text or issue?
* Who is present in the story?
* Who is named or unnamed?
* How are people described?
* People in the story are described as being in relationship to what or whom?
* What seems to be the significance of these descriptions?
* In what ways do the descriptions connect to the perceptions of people or groups in the past or present?
* In what ways do the descriptions connect to the fate of people or groups in the past or present?
* Are there any other stories, people, or events that come to mind as we encounter the text or issue at hand (i.e., headlines, everyday life, biblical texts, or the wider tradition)? Do not limit responses to Scripture.
* Is anyone's physical well-being, emotional well-being, or spiritual well-being at stake? If so, whose and why?
* Is anyone advocating for their own well-being or the well-being of someone else?

* What's at stake if there is or is not an intervention? And for whom?
* On whose side do you hope God is on, and why? Does anything seem to contradict or support your hope?
* If you had to name the presence of hate or evil, where or what is it?
* What do we need or want to know more about?

Every response to these questions shapes the way the preacher and community choose to tell the story of the world around them and text before them. They also are the seeds for considering why and how to live as more engaged people of faith.

While these are enduring questions for a process of exploration, each encounter with Scripture and the world causes more questions to emerge. They are questions grounded in the particularities of a passage of Scripture and the contemporary world around us. For practical purposes, Matthew 15:21–28 is explored in chapter 5 to imagine what these questions might be and how they may impact sermon outcomes.

Resourcing Fleshy Parts and Preaching

When the community of faith is aware of matters of the flesh, they pay attention wherever they arise. Any manner of threat or harm to a person's well-being, whether revealed in Scripture or the present times of the world, is a transgression against God-given integrity. This integrity is reflected in the creation narratives of Genesis 1 and 2, where humanity is fashioned out of dust and receives the breath of life into their nostrils. The final judgment is, "God saw everything that [God] had made, and indeed, it was very good" (Gen 1:31).

Preaching seeks to avoid contributing to ongoing bodily suffering just as much as it opens a space for the community to attend to such suffering. Sheer survival is a precursor to our ability to thrive. To be sure, some of the greatest threats to our survival stem from the disregard of human life based on how we literally take up space in the world.

The preacher is called to better understand matters of the flesh in order to be in more responsible conversation with them for preaching. This means, at minimum, they pursue a working knowledge of faith talk in conversations with resources that attend to the general structures of race, class, gender, age, abilities, and sexuality as well as the permeable, almost nonexistent borders between them as they impact our lives.

3

Taboo Conversations
Religion, Money, and Politics

Oppression upon oppression, deceit upon deceit!
They refuse to know me, says the Lord.

—Jeremiah 9:6

When we value and honor the totality of what it means to be human—spirit and flesh without bifurcation—additional demands are placed upon our actions in the world and what it means to live together. For starters, we contend with the very present corporeal needs and desires that accompany living. At a minimum, these necessities and yearnings involve food, shelter, safety, a connection to others, a volition to be well, and a desire for the transcendent in the present. All these things reside at the core of conversations about money, politics, and religion.

We make decisions about money, politics, and religion according to our personal beliefs and values, and yet these decisions are always tethered to some form of collective thinking. We act based on what we discern as significant and for whom it is best. Our processes of discernment are shaped by the people who influence us just as much as our actions impact the lives of others. Money, politics, and religion are never private matters alone, as they both are shaped by the collective community and have implications for all people. And yet we call these subjects taboo.

The conversations are not taboo because of their "private" nature. We call these conversations taboo because tensions, disagreements, and even points of agreement arise when we engage them. We open ourselves to a process of assessment when we disclose our values and actions. People assess our participation in aiding or hindering the tangibly basic needs and yearnings of others. Our acceptance and rejection of those assessments create the tensions we experience. We often urge or avoid accountability to collective well-being while justifying how our decisions do or do not impact others. Simply put, the push and pull within the conversations involve our contesting what it means to be accountable in daily decision-making.

Avoiding the conversations also means avoiding our responsibility to the most basic of human need and yearning—well-being. But to love God and neighbor inherently assumes we will practice accountability in our beliefs and actions. When actively engaging in matters of money, politics, and religion, the community of faith has the opportunity to be more accountable to collective well-being. This opportunity comes through an ongoing assessment of our values and actions. Unless we name things as they are in view of what they could be, we miss the opportunity. Naming creates a space both to acknowledge and to turn toward a more right-fitting direction for collective well-being. Naming allows us to better imagine what being accountable to beliefs and actions entails.

The movement between acknowledging and turning is an anchor in Christian traditions of confession and repentance, while naming present realities in view of alternative ones resides at the center of lament. Both preacher and community are ushered anew to the threshold of long-held traditions of confession and repentance, as they name the consequences of communal negligence in matters of collective well-being. And in doing so, lament provides the space for imagining the concrete possibilities of confession and repentance in the times at hand.

Behind and beyond the Headlines

When engaging the topics of money, religion, and politics, people often declare what they believe to be most at stake and necessary for well-being. Snapshots of our struggles around these topics often crystallize a history of actions and consequences and their impact on life on the ground. Understanding what's behind the dynamics of the snapshots helps the preacher make use of them both for acknowledging the current state of affairs and for the community's process of discerning their participation in cultivating a different world.

Tangible Matters

Public headlines echo very practical needs and desires that are often debated and then litigated. We need resources to live, economic and otherwise—*money*. Many yearn for spiritual understandings or connections with the transcendent and then order their lives and relationships around such yearnings—*religion*. As we live in community, we need to determine our general pacts for living together—*politics*. Sentiments about these practical realities at minimum quietly impact our informal agreements about how to interact with one other and at most become the site of intense conflict. While we are tempted to paint money, politics, and religion as discrete concerns, they are constantly entangled, as our headlines often attest.

In June 2020, the US news circuits covered some form of the following: "Supreme Court Says Federal Law Protects LGBTQ Workers from Discrimination."[1] Simply reading the words begins to tell us a bit about the dynamics in play. *Supreme Court says* there was a judgment delivered about a current *federal law* and its extension to the *protection* of a particular demographic of people and their labor practices (*LGBTQ workers*). Digging deeper reveals that this ruling is connected to a familiar struggle in history for a people's equal protection from discrimination. In this instance, the concern focuses on one's ability to earn wages without any obstacles grounded in references to that person's sexuality or gender identity.

The Supreme Court justices stated their opinion based on an interpretation of the Civil Rights Act of 1964, which deemed that discrimination against persons on the basis of race, ethnicity, sex, religion, or country of origin was not lawful.[2] "Civil Rights Act: How South Responds" was the headline of a *New York Times* article on July 12, 1964.[3] The 1964 ruling impacted voting rights, employment, public accommodations, and educational facilities, all of which at state levels were still marred by practices of legalized racial segregation, despite the ratification of a succession of amendments to the Constitution during and after the Reconstruction period.[4] Reactions to the 1964 legislation included a range of behaviors. Some pursued loopholes such as turning public spaces into private invitational clubs only. Others outright refused to comply with legislation by any means, violent or otherwise. Those who accepted the changes either actively acknowledged them as long overdue or were passively resigned to the new direction things were moving.

The period from July 2, 1964, to the June 2020 court decision demonstrated that such laws of the land are significant and impact our daily living and processes of recourse. And yet legal pacts and legislation can never fully eliminate the daily tensions that arise in our lived social contexts and varying social values. While headlines speak of politics and money, deeper issues of human need lie under the surface. We identify the importance of each person's need for safety, food, shelter, well-being, and a way of life undergirded by access to resources and procedures that ensure such access. One's ability to access a viable livelihood remains in jeopardy post–June 2020, just as it did post–July 1964. Rulings do not cure that jeopardy or change the sentiment of a nation. But they do provide more stable channels for action and support against such discrimination.

Naming discrimination creates a different set of expectations around our interactions, but we still must contend with the way our values impact our interactions. Who is able to *earn* a living without impediment in a society that runs on social and monetary capital says something of how our actions align with valuing the needs of all people. The capacity to earn a living without impediment addresses whether we believe some people are entitled to such rights while others are not. The questions are, Who is eligible for such protection? Who has the ability to decide and barter such eligibility? The greater clarity we gain about our values during these tensions makes way for revising our social pacts.

Religion and cultural values and the battle of powers within them impact the ways we both arrive at our social agreements and litigate them. The ruling about LGBTQ labor rights is not disconnected from the headline "Court Affirms Bakeshop Owner's

Refusal to Sell Wedding Cake to Gay Couple Due to Evangelical Religious Objections."[5] The history of aligning the concerns of Christian faith with legislative decisions around what are and are not discriminatory practices cannot be lost here. Some strands of the Christian faith claim religious freedom in order to argue for and against equal rights protections,[6] health care issues,[7] and marriage rights. Actions on the ground demonstrate that religious freedoms can be treated and legislated unevenly.

We witness this unevenness play out in headlines in subtle and not-so-subtle ways. For instance, "France Will Still Ban Islamic Face Coverings Even after Making Masks Mandatory."[8] The bodies of Muslim women and how they were adorned in public were being legislated. Ironically, in 2020, in the midst of the COVID-19 pandemic, all French citizens were mandated to wear face coverings, which was in direct conflict with the safety concerns expressed regarding concealed faces, cited in the previous Muslim face-covering mandate.

Each of these instances is founded in sentiments that result in limiting the humanity of someone else and subsequently diminishing the legitimacy of their needs and desires. Those needs may include a person's wages or their desire to mark a partnership with a ritual. Such sentiments are lodged in the structural and systemic mechanisms of society and impact how we live together in the world.

Tangible Tensions

Multiple contestations of religious and cultural values are carried out in the public square. Religious values cannot easily be disentangled from cultural values that impact the rhythms of our daily lives and livelihood. And we witness this entanglement in our conversations about money, politics, and religions.

Again, the headlines used earlier are only stand-ins for any given headline that may lead us to the same conclusions. Often we leverage the most basic of human yearnings and needs into items we exchange, hoard, and forcibly regulate. They become commodities, showing how we are often guided by fear, scarcity, greed, and threat. We move these commodities at the discretion of some and to the exclusion of others. They are privatized and negotiable with minimum regard for how our decisions impact our neighbors. In the most extreme scenarios, our neighbors and their needs are moved and negotiated away. This disregard for neighbor includes their access to medical care, information, home ownership, public worship practices, safety, nourishment, and so many other things.

Deep emotions and tensions arise in these conversations because we recognize something very personal is at stake in our discussions and decision-making. The same histories of power and privilege that play out in the fleshy parts of our interactions, as far as who matters most, also are at work in our pursuit of what we most need and desire.

Furthermore, when our yearnings for the transcendent are most aligned with or capable of swaying our social agreements, religion itself becomes a type of social capital. It is a social capital that influences our spoken and unspoken social agreements. These social agreements impact our access to and experience of the most basic of human needs and desires. The semiotic relationship between our religious and cultural values can limit or make more possible our abilities to survive and thrive in the world at large, as the relationship influences how we make determinations about what or who is most meaningful in our shared existence.

Privileging those things named as Christian values has played a palpable role in our debates, legislation, and outcomes in the West. The preacher and community are called to critically assess both the root cause of conflicts in matters of money, politics, and religion and the way their values become obstacles or pathways to a just world. The risks are multidimensional if we do not.

Tangible Risks

Avoiding these challenging conversations risks the same past and present outcomes that result from diminishing the humanity of someone else, as their sanctioning is often intertwined with faith claims. We view the needs, desires, and equitable participation of people in the world as options in an ongoing way. The lack of protection around living wages, segregation, Jim and Jane Crow laws, practices of desensitization in mass incarceration, voter suppression, and sanctioned acts of genocide such as the Holocaust and transatlantic slave trade infers something about how we perceive the most basic of human needs and desires as both optional and negotiable. Religion, and specifically Christianity, has also been used to justify or mobilize against each of these concerns.

Pulling back the curtain of the world also pulls back the curtain on people of faith. Addressing the open disparagement of human needs creates its own risks for both preacher and community. New questions collide with old methods. Risk entails dismantling claims, texts, and beliefs with which we've grown far too comfortable. Risk means venturing into the uncharted territory of something more life affirming. We risk being confronted by the possibility of our own failures. Our complicity in interpreting the faith tradition in ways that downplay the legitimacy of basic human needs and desires may readily be exposed.

Earnest reflection is vulnerable reflection. It creates the possibility of enlivening the contours of discipleship for the here and now. For these reasons, we risk exposing the ways we have not been accountable to what is most needed in sustaining the lives of our neighbor, even as we pull back the layers of our world. We are better able to assume these risks if we both understand them as part of life with God and have a language to talk about what we are pursuing in faith terms.

Recovering and honoring basic human needs and desires in society, as opposed to treating them as commodities, are not impossible. Our ability to turn away from our practices of commodification and toward new ways of being together is dependent upon naming the ongoing risks we face if we do not live in new ways. The preacher helps the community explore the tradition in order to name and address the current state of affairs for more life-sustaining outcomes.

Exploring Faith

We turn to the faith tradition and remember that our ability to live together in more just ways depends on our ability to acknowledge the ways we have not honored human needs. The very acts of naming, acknowledging, and doing differently are the core of Christian traditions of lament, confession, and repentance. But the latter two hinge on the ability to acknowledge something is going awry—lament.

Preaching that relies on the tradition of lament to inform its frameworks of interpretation and its methods calls out those things that the community does and does not regularly recognize as egregious. The lament tradition also attends to the sorrow-inducing realities. The community enters a space to push past the veneer of "This is just the way things are," for this veneer affirms our silence in instances where we should be crying out on behalf of others. Together, preacher and community begin the work of leaving no stone unturned as faithful practice. This faithful practice is a guide for engaging the world, Scripture, and tradition.

Tangible Changes

Matters of money, politics, and religion are not simply about those buzzwords in and of themselves.[9] Instead, the sermon invites the community into a process of discerning and intuiting matters at the core of money, politics, and religion. Part of that invitation is helping the community recognize that these are not extracurricular activities and concerns for people of faith; thinking around and responding to human needs and desires are par for the course as persons of faith. The issues behind these words need to permeate a message in multiple ways to help the community discern its role in our social agreements.

With this in mind, the preacher is attentive to recasting the story of faith and the story of this world in order to make space for an engaged practice that calls forth God's futures in our midst. Our proclivity toward commodifying the needs and yearnings of our neighbors has led to our participation in dishonoring the sanctity of all life, as it perceives resources, safety, connections, and mutual existence as options instead of being nonnegotiable. This also means showing clearly how we have made faith itself into a commodity by our actions.

Acknowledging faith as a commodity means exposing the places where those things we do in the name of faith have become less about our ongoing connection to God and more about our connections to power. How do we recognize these places? These are the places where we disregard and violate the most basic of human needs and yearnings. In other words, the ethic of preaching is guided by the assumption that anything that contributes to the demise of our neighbors in the name of religion is not a faithful response but rather is rigidly aligned with behaviors and practices that cling to supremacy or faithlessness. This rigidity expresses more about our sporadic disconnection from an awareness of God and neighbor than it does about the certainty of our connection to God.[10] So, all we do in the name of religion also needs to come to center stage for earnest interrogation.

The preacher now surveys the world, Scripture, and the faith tradition with at least one critical question in mind: What does it look like when we value the most basic of human needs and desires as holy things we are called to honor and protect? The pursuit of the question does not swiftly move the community to joy-filled or tidy resolutions. Instead, it illuminates how our inability to acknowledge the fullness of human life falls short of God's intent. Similarly, the question calls us to imagine, even in our finite abilities, what God's justice looks like.

Tangible Faith Talk

Christian faith traditions have long held space for lament—even if preaching and worship practices do not always make use of it. Of course, we acknowledge that there will be times when we will not fully have the words to capture the complexities of what we most witness and feel. For instance, we know the feeling of the inadequacy of words when circumstances around us evoke deep grief, outrage, or joy. Nevertheless, we try to find words that resonate to mark the presence of an experience. Lament through preaching has a confessional tone.[11]

The push here is not to hide the uncomfortable things or pretend as though they do not exist. The preacher and community acknowledge the negligence and wrongful action toward human needs and desires, the death and sorrow that result from these sins, and the genuine inquiry of where God's presence may be located or where God is leading us to in the midst of it all. Often lament is the stumbling block within preaching when we are not comfortable raising issues of sadness, outrage, and doubt or even questioning because they seem to be antithetical to belief. There are no tidy and easy answers in the face of experiencing grief, loss, or wrongdoing. Necessary catharsis and faithlessness are not the same. Lament does not seek to hide the depths of human emotions and despair. Lament through preaching recaptures lamentation as a faith-filled act. Luke Powery has offered one of the most extensive treatments of lament and preaching to date and recovers the Spirit as the one who enables lament.[12]

Lament is an action that trusts that God and the community can withstand and absorb the outrage and grief at hand without cowering away or being too small to hold it. Hymnody has often held the connection of lament and hope together without contradiction. The lyrics "Up above my head / I hear music in the air. / There must be a God somewhere" affirms God's presence just as much as "Come by here, my Lord. Come by here. / Somebody's crying, Lord. Come by here" affirms God is moved by what has moved us to weeping. Lament produces courageous postures of vulnerability, not postures of faithlessness and resignation. We can trace these postures through the book of Lamentations, through the weeping prophet Jeremiah and the wailing company of women, and through the cries of Psalm 22:1 that echo in Jesus's words as he is in the throes of being crucified in an unjust world: "My God, my God, why have you forsaken me?"

Lament in preaching names the way people, their needs, and their desires are not valued but treated as commodities. Lament in preaching also acknowledges the places where the community contributes to those practices of violation instead of making ways for better and more just practices. The consistent call here is for people of faith to pursue these dynamics in the worlds of the text and in today's world with more honesty and less sanitization. It is in this call that both the challenges and the possibilities emerge for preaching.

Christine Smith offers that if preaching is to attend to the radical evils of this world, preaching itself must be radical. This radicalness lies in the work of leading a community into honest reflection, which then leads to radical responses.[13] Part of this honest reflection includes weeping and confession as pathways to radical resistance and new futures. Once something is spoken or named, it is then opened up to be held, interrogated, or vetted by the community around us.[14]

Before we are able to turn away from one way of living and toward a different way of living together, the community must acknowledge the most undesirable and broken ways of living together. That acknowledgment is the work of lament. Lament is the means by which we expose and name what should not be in order to make way for alternative futures and, more explicitly, participate in creating those futures. To turn away from one thing and to another thing is the most basic call of Christian repentance. We cannot skip over lament in the process any more than we can skip over the things that are lament worthy. This means we cannot skip over matters of money, politics, and religion in preaching—because they are places that expose our faithlessness and cry out for a more just future.

Tangible Preaching Possibilities

The preacher keeps in mind collective accountability when using lament as an interpretive framework. The goal is the possibility of more generative outcomes from the faith tradition for the world today. The sermon helps move the community toward accountability in their actions through earnest reflection on the world, the tradition, and Scripture. The preacher attends to dynamics of resources, agreements about how we live together, and the influence of religion in that mix. The work is just as uncomfortable and stretching as it is earnest, and so are the practices of message development that support it.

The preacher's work is to model through preaching what faith-filled witness might look like in the world. This includes acknowledging the anguish and sorrow, naming all that's against God's greatest hopes, and turning toward those things that are in pursuit of God's greatest hopes. The sermon form names and turns toward alternative futures or endings. But such a form is only supported by the pathways of the text and world we pursue and how we engage the preaching imagination to ask questions and follow such pathways.

First, neither lament nor the repentance that follows is viewed as a personal practice alone. Lament and repentance are corporate practices of the community and society also. Communal practices include both collective and personal participation. So in preaching, we search to hold the personal aspects and communal aspects of lament and repentance together.

Practically, this might mean we acknowledge Hannah's personal prayers and sorrow about her barrenness in the temple before God (1 Sam 1:9–11). And we also acknowledge and express outrage over the social agreements that made her fertility status an impediment to accessing present and future resources and communal belonging. The crying out of one person may lead to us making confessions about our spoken and unspoken social agreements. And that process of naming provides a space for collective discernment around turning away from harmful existing agreements in order to live differently. In Hannah's case, how would her life be different if women's access to resources and social status were not understood to be tied to their reproductive capacity? How would her life be different in a world of reproductive justice?

Second, lament as an interpretive framework might be applied to any given text and not limited to those texts we readily perceive as holding characteristics of lament. Some Scripture passages have characteristics of lament in their content or form. We might think of books such as Lamentations, various Psalms, the infamous weeping prophet Jeremiah, passages within Isaiah, and so on, but here we acknowledge something more of the possibilities of frameworks of lament beyond those texts. Lament provides a gateway into some of the most difficult texts of Scripture without the need to spiritually moralize them or save the face of the faith tradition through their justification.

Justification is not required if the intent is to name what is going awry for the sake of something more. Instead of justification, we acknowledge and attend to some things we have otherwise given tidy endings and ignored. For example, we raise a different set of questions when Joshua leads the encampment of Israel into the promised land with the armed guard and priests at the forefront of the procession and then *burns every living thing* within the walls of Jericho (Josh 1–6). Every living thing would include the lives of people alongside creaturely beings being destroyed in the name of faith. The preacher now has to determine what is at stake in the world today if they preach in unequivocal affirmation of these actions in the text. We still live in times in which groups of people are victims of genocide and caught in the web of war. The community knows the precariousness of the world in which they live just as much as the preacher.

The preacher seeks to illuminate the world and the text in ways that push through our desensitization to dishonoring human need and longing in both. We must have a willingness to see these failures in the world around us as people try to figure out life with God and one another. And we are required to see these same failures in history—including the histories of the biblical worlds and faith tradition. Alternative questions emerge as we maintain an awareness of privileging human life while acknowledging the proclivity of religion to become an idolatrous partner in the work of dishonoring and commodifying human life.

The preacher seeks to be as specific as possible for the most concrete translations to the process of sermon development. The following questions keep the concerns of collective well-being and accountability in mind:

* What basic human need or longing is being protected or denied (i.e., safety, food, connection to others, connection to God, etc.)?
* What is the impact of these things being protected or denied? Who is most affected?
* What emotions and feelings come to the surface when you reflect on your previous responses?
* What social pacts or agreements led to these outcomes?
* What assumptions or values (religious or otherwise) are constraining the choices and outcomes?

* Why does or doesn't this ending contribute to a flourishing and just world?
* If it does not contribute to flourishing, what would a just ending look like?
* Who and what could have changed the course of this story?
* If something has gone awry, where, how, and by whom is it acknowledged as going awry?
* What social pacts or regulations in your community or the world come to mind that hinge on diminishing the needs or longing for connection of someone or a group?
* What final interpretations of this passage would exacerbate these scenarios? What might the outcomes look like?
* What final interpretations of this passage would help transform these scenarios? What might the outcomes look like?

These are enduring questions. And just as with fleshy matters, the particularities of the text and world open us up to additional questions when we seek to name what is awry in the hope of something new emerging. For practical purposes, Judges 11:28–40 is explored in chapter 5 to demonstrate what those questions might look like and how they might impact sermon development. Our intent is an ongoing posture of learning to think and discern alongside texts with a commitment to honoring human needs and yearning for connection at all costs.

Resourcing Taboo
Conversations and Preaching

Giving attention to matters of money, religion, and politics is an engaged practice of faith that recognizes being collectively accountable to beliefs and their implications for concrete outcomes in the world at hand. As preaching calls the community away from treating the most basic of our needs and desires as negotiable, it creates an opening to imagine concretely what honoring human needs and desires looks like. Lament, alongside repentance, creates opportunities for a community to name what it claims it most believes and then pursue these beliefs through concrete exploration and practice.

The community may find themselves being called away from stagnation and complicity and called to social action as informed by collective study, prayer, and discernment. In supporting this work, the preacher and the community expand their resources to include conversations with those who may engage in things such as political theology, community organizing, economics, public health, policy making, history, and interfaith engagement.

The preacher's hope is to make a space for the community to imagine alternative futures and ways of living together. The path forward comes through a willingness to engage the text and world in a way that acknowledges and interrogates those things that make us unconformable, might highlight disagreement, and cause tension ahead of any resolutions. These are the pathways that affirm and recover our connectedness to God and each other while avoiding the foil of religious rigidity, for these pathways are marked by an awareness of our connection to God and neighbor alongside God's generative and creative disclosure of more just ways forward.

4

Struggles for Belonging
Environment, Land, and Borders

For the creation waits with eager longing for the revealing of the children of God.

—Romans 8:19

Until now, we have explicitly considered what it means to be aware of and initiate love practice with other people. My immediate neighbors next door, down the road, and across the way are of concern just as much as my exponential neighbors in the market, down the river, and across the ocean. Without qualification, all humanity is our neighbor. Our attitudes, beliefs, and actions impact our neighbor. The ways I vote, shop, travel, fund initiatives, talk at the dinner table, or do so many other things eventually have implications for the life of someone else. As we acknowledge what has gone awry in our midst and the radical evils that plague us and turn toward alternative ways of living together, we demonstrate our greater awareness of God and neighbor. A greater awareness of our neighbor means awareness of all neighbors.

Our conflicts and search for resolutions around land, environment, and borders signal deeper conversations about our ability, or lack thereof, to be in relationship with *all* that neighbors us. Our living in fractured or continuous relationship with our neighbor sways so much more than human relationships. Our neighbors in this sense include the nonhuman aspects of creation as well as humans. Righting our relationship with our neighbor is righting our relationship with the entire creation.

Participation toward a more just creation impacts all that is sustained by the divine life force in the world. Righting a relationship with the entire creation assumes the created integrity of every living thing that dwells within and sustains this vast space.[1] Acknowledging created integrity means we also must acknowledge our transgressions against this integrity wherever they occur. We disregard the sanctity of life by asserting that someone or something does not belong or does not right to a home—most often through domination and possession.

Love practice at its core is about how we understand our relationships to God and neighbor. Our framing of these relationships impacts how we attend to them. The community of faith that engages matters of land, environment, and borders for more transformative outcomes reframes what it means to be in a more right-fitting relationship with the creation of God. Righting our relationship to creation entails pursuing different ways of dwelling within and among it. In this pursuit, the preacher must determine how to reclaim our interactions with the world as a relationship that relies on deep awareness, mutual dependence, and stewardship.

Behind and beyond the Headlines

Public conversations about land, the environment, and borders often focus on issues related to citizenship, immigration, resources, property ownership, creeping-crawling beings, climate shifts, and various facets of the natural world. The subjects of their content are interconnected. Power dynamics, such as those discussed previously, cause the interconnectedness of some aspects of creation to be impacted more readily than others. Pushing through surface-level language about these subjects helps the community determine how their collective discernment will impact wider social agreements and actions—both in explicit policy and in lived commitments.

Tangible Matters

From 2016 to 2017, the Sioux people of the Standing Rock Reservation challenged a private natural gas and petroleum corporation in a standoff that also involved the US federal government and agencies such as the US Army Corps of Engineers.[2] Tensions rose as militarized contractors took up opposing positions to Sioux inhabitants of the land and their allies. The conflict arose over the extension of a one-thousand-mile-long oil pipeline through tribal lands. The Sioux people determined the line to be a threat to both the waters that supplied them and the sacred lands on which they resided. A nonviolent encampment organized by youths was met with both symbolized and literal violent force in the forms of riot gear, frigid water, and physical arrests. The outcries around the event were not simply about the optics, the actions, or the moment at hand.

These events echoed back to the United States' history, when Indigenous peoples were forcibly displaced from their land and threatened, while the resources that sustained them were co-opted. This situation at Standing Rock was yet another example of the legacy of actions in the United States, such as those in the events of the Trail of Tears and others; this event was no less strategic or violent but was more subtle. This occupation jeopardized the land and the people's ongoing ability to sustain their lives. We witnessed the intersections of livelihood, threats to it, and rights of possession at the site of Standing Rock Reservation. Standing Rock became an example of the historical practices of colonization and its repercussions, including infringement on resources and the accompanying assumptions about rights to resources.

The event is not an isolated one. This history is played out in many places throughout the world. Natural resources, land, and water, function as a type of currency that brings proximity to power. For instance, blood diamonds receive their name because foreign powers and local regimes made use of African communities for mining diamonds.[3] These mining practices relied on war and uncompensated or poorly compensated human labor at the great expense of human life through death and through horribly deteriorated living conditions. This cycle is just one part of the continent's history of foreign occupation and exploitation, in collusion with local regimes, of both human and natural resources.

The issues of Standing Rock and blood diamonds are not separate from those raised around fracking for oil and gas across the United States, especially in economically depressed areas. Those who oppose the practice raise concerns about the pollutants fracking emits into the environment, posing a threat to the quality of air, soil, and water, and therefore, to the inhabitants of the areas. Its proponents highlight that it provides financial resources and employment to those who might not otherwise have them.

These matters are just as much about who or what is involved as they are about how we acquire what we've determined we need and want. People purchase jewelry continents and oceans away from the mining sites. People purchase oil and gas for fueling households, travel, and businesses. And the way we sustain our daily operations leads to conversations about irreversible climate change, rainforest depletion, and poor ecological health found in headlines such as "Temperatures in an Arctic Siberian Town Hit 100 Degrees, a New High."[4] Cycles of demand and fulfillment cause exponential ripples in the world. The issue at hand is how the pursuit of sustaining our residency impacts the rest of creation.

How we've maintained residency is linked to the history of erecting and maintaining divisions of land, air, and water masses. These divisions are both visible and invisible borders. All that resides within and outside borders is subject to the alignment of opportunity and vulnerability. The alignment of opportunity and vulnerability impacts policies, decisions, and actions regarding property lines, territorial demarcations, citizenship, immigration, migration, refugee seeking, extinction, trade, and so much more. Proximity to power in the alignment of opportunity and vulnerability makes all the difference in how we fare in relationship to space and place. But we all live with the outcomes.

Tangible Tensions

The collective struggles of all who reside in this world are impacted by matters of environment, land, and borders. We are limited to telling the story of God's vast creation through the lens of our human patterns and their impact on the world.[5] Simply put, we do not know how history would be told "if the rocks cried out."

But even our limited human vantage point mirrors the ways we selfishly center on ourselves as individuals and communities when engaging all that is near and far from us in the world. We have prioritized ourselves above all other life-forms, even as we have not honored all human life equally.

Our tendency toward domination of one another impacts the interconnected web in which we live. Our power-seeking actions claim a right to invade, occupy, and excavate or withhold resources without restraint. We lay claim on all that neighbors us, including the created world. As we lay claim to land, sea, and sky, we also lay claim to those things that sustain our neighbors and their needs. Our strategies of commodifying and dishonoring life without collective accountability lead to manipulating the resources of creation. We use them for our purposes, disturbing habitats and endangering the equilibrium of the ecosystem.

The reverberation of these patterns of manipulating the wider ecology is centered on who has the greater ability to persuade or force and who or what is most vulnerable. Our literal actions visibly claim, "You do not belong, you do not have the right to belong, and you are mine." We most often associate *belonging* with "belonging to" in terms of ownership. Every day, headline or not, we witness our privileging power alongside possession. Our constant infringement on all life-forms causes unnaturally seismic unrest for all that dwells herein. The most vulnerable of creation live with the disproportionate consequences of our patterns.

We live amid struggles for grounding and rest. Belonging is just as much about space and place as it is about relationship. Belonging is about affinity and connectedness. The opportunity to be sustained, grounded, and received is a part of having a place of belonging to or with another. We attempt to name these things when we use language like "being at home" or "finding a place or home." To be sustained, grounded, and received is the opposite of disruption, displacement, and extinction.

We live amid the struggles for the recognition that every living thing was created with integrity; this inherent integrity is connected to the capacity and right to belong here and be in relationship. We are unable to uphold the rights of something or someone to be sustained and grounded in this vast creation if we do not honor their integrity as a part of this creation.

We are mutually dependent. No single human stands alone at the center of the human story and no human is the center of creation's story outside the rest of creation. But our emphasis on power and domination claims otherwise. Care of creation, equitable land use, and just management of borders are matters that lead to struggle and disagreement. The preacher's task will include speaking to these matters in clear and tangible ways.

Tangible Risks

At present, opportunities for sustenance and stability in our interconnected web often depend on access to power. We reap the devastation in wars over land possession, conquests, forced migrations, and natural resource depletion, which lead to the extinction of wildlife and people. We also reap these devastations in sometimes more subtle but no less violent ways, such as when we limit access to resources by way of food deserts, contaminated water supplies, unaffordable housing or the absence of housing, policies on immigration, definitions of citizenship, and public policies that impact it all.

Without intervention, we will continue to weaponize the ecosystem against ourselves and itself, reduce viable habitats, use resources and procure without throttle, and increase the level of forced displacement, migration, and extinction. History has proven as much. We risk our more expedient destruction instead of our quite literal collective salvation.

Living in more just ways with the wider creation means attending to the volatile repercussions of our past and existing power struggles. If we do not attend to these repercussions, both our human and nonhuman worlds will continue to suffer. We cannot dissolve or correct the systems upon which we have come to rely without reaping the inertia of the violence that sustains them.[6] We have not lived well and responsibly in this interconnected space. Power and domination do not secede themselves, nor will the societal structures and practices that rely on them simply go away.

Righting our relationships within and to creation is not about easy answers or uncomplicated sorting. It is a direct confrontation of our practices of possession and consumerism. These are conversations about what we eat, how we get food, from where we get food, and by what means. We are now called to consider how and where we get clothing, technologies, fuel, and our power sources. These are conversations that carefully consider the ongoing legitimacy of land and area possession while recognizing a disproportionate ability of some to possess over and against or at the expense of others. These are matters of deep entanglement and complicity.

Changes hinge on our ability to experiment and pursue difficult conversations that when done well and with integrity will likely upend our patterns of living. The questions raised by matters of environment, land, and borders are those that address collective and personal responsibility in a space where our final fate is impacted by the whole.

Exploring Faith

Moving communities of faith to more engaged and responsible practices regarding all matters of belonging requires a deepening awareness of our relationship to all creation and our impact on it. The preacher's work becomes that of more closely narrating the story and tradition of faith alongside matters of belonging. More specifically, this means attending to respecting the inherent integrity of, mutual dependence on, and responsibility to all that resides in the world. This involves reframing our relationship with creation beyond domination and subjugation toward communion and stewardship. But even more so, it requires recovering, restoring, and sustaining creation here and now as a concern of God.

The simple call is for communities of faith to live the assumptions that reside at the core of the tradition, beginning with the belief that life is worth salvaging and sustaining. The tradition's narratives are anchored by God's radical love practice that makes way for creation being saved from the finality of death and destruction, and this means not simply part of the creation but the entire creation. If we retain the language of salvation, this becomes an opportunity to be more specific about what salvation means for whom and by what means while emphasizing interconnectedness. Romans 8 describes the entire creation groaning and waiting for the children of God to be revealed in order that it might be saved. This hoped-for outcome is not isolated to a future age of an unrevealed heaven and earth (Rom 8:18–25). Instead, attending to the groans of creation is something to which people of faith are called to do here and now precisely because of God's salvific work.

Tangible Changes

Supporting more engaged participation here and now relies on at least one major shift in understanding our relationship to creation. This change involves moving away from constantly distancing ourselves from the world at hand through otherworldly and future-oriented outlooks. The unintended consequence of focusing on otherworldly and future outlooks is escapism from accountability—turning our backs on the real conditions in which we live. Attending to this world as a current home that is not to be ignored opens a different conversation about what attentiveness to this space means in consideration of our ongoing relationship with God.[7] It also requires the reconsideration of the question, "Who is my neighbor?"

The constant overemphasis on an otherworldly future glory diminishes the internal struggles for belonging within the world at hand. It relegates life and our experiences to being temporary and of minimum significance. For instance, when demonstrating the veracity of salvation, Christian people of faith often say, "We are in the world but not of the world," or they claim they are "saved to" a future glory and home with the coming of a new heaven and earth as the present ones pass away. Shifting away from an overemphasis on a future new life and day when all things will be made right in the "by and by" does not necessitate denying these promises. But it does mean probing more deeply what we're saved from and saved to here and now.

Being saved from something and to something new implies having an awareness of our communion with God. Such awareness impacts the way we live in the present. And more specifically, this awareness means caring for the rest of creation as we live among it. With an attentiveness to the here and now, promises of a new heaven and new earth extend into the existing ones and are not ex nihilo replacements removed from our current space and place. In other words, life-rescuing and life-sustaining activities have implications for the here and now and affect our neighbors here and now. Herein lies a shift in our focus on where we belong and to whom we mutually belong.

In the most plainly stated way, "What if this is all we've got?" And what if we are called to the promises of salvation here and now? Those promises involve rescuing us all unto life instead of death. For some, the idea of renewed heavens and earth coming forth from the existing ones will feel radical if not heretical. More than whether or not these are actual occurrences, what remains important here is that we have nothing to lose if we practice the value at the core of the Christian hope for renewed life. Those would be practices of life-renewing activity. What do we have to lose by doing what saves us from self-destruction? Nothing. But we have everything to lose if we only engage this world as though it is not where we belong.

Focusing on *these* heavens and this earth as a space to which we belong demands an openness to what is required for sustaining such belonging. We attend to the existing earth and heavens and the deeply situated tensions of belonging that arise in our midst because there is a sense of home that the entire creation must be reconciled to in order for life to be renewed.

This hope for renewal is not "out there" but tangibly connected to collective accountability in this space. This renewal is an accountability to all that neighbors us. We are situated alongside the vast diversities of this creation at any given moment. Shifting the perspective to cultivating this space for the renewal of all creation embeds a different type of accountability within our love practice as people of faith. These attitudes and actions reclaim communion and stewardship as opposed to dominating and subduing a temporal domain and its inhabitants. Furthermore, we might understand ourselves operating in economies where gifting and exchange are our currencies through the outlook of plentitude or abundance[8] instead of commodifying through dominant mindsets of purchasing and possession and the outlook of scarcity.

The engaged community of faith centers on the question, What does it mean if the world we've cocreated is in part the world of our future inheritance also—including its relationships and sustainability? This question reframes the community of faith's considerations for interacting with every living thing in our midst as a neighbor with whom we are in a mutually dependent relationship. These can be ongoing relationships of supplanting, displacement, and extinction—or relationships of survival, sustenance, and life sponsoring.

Tangible Faith Talk

The actual rite or sacrament of Communion provides one point of entry for changing our course of relationship with creation here and now. Fellowship and salvific activity reside at the core of the ritual's themes. And here is the opportunity to be more specific about the meaning and possibilities of those themes in the midst of struggles for belonging.

The ritual of communion involves an invitation to a table of fellowship. The invitation assumes a place of connection not just to fellow participants in that space but to those who have participated in the past and who will participate in the future. The ritual assumes belonging to a wider fellowship—a group connected in relationship. The relational connections of this greater community are anchored by a summons to awareness.[9]

Memory is the mechanism of this summons.[10] The Communion cup and bread conjure a greater memory about the story of faith. The gathering recalls that they have been saved from the finality of death and destruction, saved to life and sustenance, and saved by a radical love practice. The love practice at the center of the Communion story is anchored in the belief that God so loved the world that God came as an incarnational holy being and lived in our midst so that there might be life everlasting. Jesus suffered a violent death by actual hands in this world after living in a way that sought to sustain the capacity of life within it. The most radical love practice was a commitment to life amid the most destructive and deteriorating conditions of the creation at hand.

In the midst of enacting this grand memory, there is a call to assess how we are or are not participating in this awareness. The community is called to survey its worthiness before consumption in order to not reap the judgment of participating in an unworthy way. Anything that obstructs awareness at the table risks the exact opposite of the lifesaving activity it recognizes; it risks the possibility of premature death.[11] And God gives the judgment. So sins are confessed, and prayers of forgiveness are offered before consumption. The awareness of what it means to be saved to life from death by radical love practice assumes accountability in one's way of living.

The final call at the table is to remember salvific activity until the culmination of its appearance in Jesus's return. Communion conjures the (re)memory[12] that God came into the world to sustain the capacity of life within this created world, not outside of it; it was not an otherworldly activity disengaged from the creation at hand. The movement between memory and (re)memory keeps us close to the awareness of life-sustaining activity.

Many strands of the tradition have used the ritual to emphasize the exclusionary nature of belonging to this fellowship of belief. This exclusionary emphasis is on confessing belief in Jesus in a particular way and especially in regard to being personally saved from death and damnation. But the turning point occurs when the community uses its memory to extend table fellowship in creation here and now. This extension happens through lived awareness of the capacity of radical love practice to rescue us from death and secure us to the viability of life. The table is just as much, if not more, about the collective salvaging of creation as it is about securing personal salvation. For there is no personal without the communal.

Communion is both a confession and a calling. The community bears witness that salvaging life both happened and continues to happen. They commit to an ongoing participation in what honors the viability of life, not simply naming a distant and past action of God. Mass conversions are not the emphasis. Participating in what saves us from our own destruction is the call. That means actually engaging in lifesaving practices that confront the literal ongoing perils of death and destruction that uproot and displace life.[13] These are practices that extend the capacity of life here in this place. These are matters of care and stewardship, and these are matters of salvation. Life confronting death perpetuated by radical evil is salvation. To be in communion with God is to be in communion with the creation of God.

Tangible Preaching Possibilities

Preaching out of frameworks that affirm communion is both to confess and to summon. Such preaching calls forth the ongoing participation in what honors the viability of life, not simply naming a distant and past action of God. That means engaging in lifesaving practices that confront the literal ongoing perils of unnecessary death and displacement. These are practices that extend the capacity of life or salvation here in this world. These matters of salvation are anchored by practices of care and stewardship.

First, preaching within this framework assumes that *life confronting death through radical love practice is the way of salvation.* To attend to an awareness of God's saving acts on behalf of all creation means attending to the places where those saving acts have not been fully realized. This lack of realization is evidenced in all the ways in which creation still searches for a belonging and a place of home as it forcibly migrates, is displaced, and even is rendered extinct. The preacher pays attention to these realities in Scriptures and in the world today.

The core matters behind our conversations regarding land, environment, and even citizenship highlight our struggles for belonging. Belonging is about a state of being connected and in relationship without breach. Belonging conjures a sense of being in relationship with something or someone. It's just as much about a sense of home as it is having one's presence and place affirmed in the midst of another. To be clear, every sermon will not be about the environment, sustainability, immigration, citizenship, or land division. But the preacher's awareness of all these matters will impact when they engage them in conversation and highlight our mutual dependence on one another and the entire creation for ongoing survival.

Second, preaching makes clear the claim that to be in communion with God is to be in communion with the creation of God. This means preaching takes opportunities to highlight matters of interconnectedness and accountability. The emphasis is placed on attending to what an awareness of God brings about in our relationships with one another. Beyond lamenting or naming what has gone awry, an awareness of God opens us to a creative and regenerating love practice that sustains life instead of destroying it. These engaged practices attend to the breaches within the world that prevent mutual sustenance and grounding in this place. To live in breach with creation is the sin to be named.

Third, preaching reminds us that all that neighbors us is our neighbor, both human and nonhuman. Preaching recalls the same creation God spoke into existence in Genesis, the many creaturely things nestled inside of it, and the earth out of which humanity was fashioned. The sermon invites the community into conversations of actionable responsibility. It calls forward the recognition that this place of dwelling and its inhabitants are not our possessions. Rather, we are in relationship with them and have a responsibility to care for them instead of conquering and depleting them.

Fostering a deeper awareness of all that neighbors us and our struggles for belonging can show up in a myriad of ways within preaching. For example, we might focus on how we attend to the human characters in Scripture and their pursuit of belonging and experience of displacement. We may also focus on how we attend to creaturely and noncreaturely things in the text, especially when lifting up themes of human ownership, land use, and consumption of resources.

With struggles for belonging in view, the preacher seeks to be more accountable to how their claims land in the wider world. They contend with the issues of forced migration and extinction in the text because such concerns are part of the ongoing events in our world—be they wars, climate change, occupation, invasion, hurricanes, earthquakes, floods, and the like. They recognize flattened parallels between the text,

God's will and judgment, and the forces of natural creation lack nuance and do not account for our full interconnectedness in creation. Similarly, as our natural habitats and resources are constantly displaced, we may give greater attention to our mutual dependence on them. For instance, the wilderness is often painted as untenable and harsh within Scripture, and yet we also witness it being a place of sustenance in the narratives of Hagar, the children of Israel during their exodus, and John the Baptist.

Finally, whatever the approach, the one goal is not to attend solely to the hope of a future renewal of creation and future banquet meal with God and resurrected others at the expense of attending to the renewal of creation and communion with God and one another in the present. The following are enduring questions the community of faith may ask when exploring Scripture and the world:

* How many different aspects of creation can you name (e.g., animals, trees, rocks, streams, bodies of water, people, etc.)?
* What are those parts of creation doing? How are they interconnected?
* Who or what is being misplaced and displaced, and by what or whom?
* Who or what is at home or assumed to be at home? Why does this matter?
* Where do we witness the responsibility for our neighbors or the rejection of our neighbors, and what is the result?
* What is important about having a sense of home and place? How do our actions prevent or provide for such a

space, whether we are thinking of human or nonhuman creation?

* What is the nature of relationships we encounter (e.g., mutuality, possession, abuse, care, sustenance, etc.)?
* Where do we find the most discomfort in naming God's presence in these relationships?
* What outcomes could lead to jeopardizing someone or something?
* What does being rescued from destruction and saved to life require?
* What would it take to cooperatively sustain life?

Each encounter with Scripture and our world causes more questions about communion and belonging to emerge. For practical purposes, Genesis 16 and 2:8–21 are explored in the next chapter to demonstrate what those questions might be and how they might impact sermon development.

Resourcing Struggles for Belonging and Preaching

In attending to the struggle for belonging, the community is called to consider how interactions with one aspect of creation impact the rest of creation in multiple ways. Here the call is to simply consider what being saved from death and demise and saved to life means in very tangible ways for the entire creation. These considerations usher the community toward more engaged faith practices that recognize our mutual dependence and responsibility to each other and the wider creation.

Our being in relationship with God without breach entails being in relationship with God's entire creation without breach as we respect the created integrity of all that dwells herein. The community of faith seeks conversation partners in areas such as ecotheology, environmental ethics, sociology, immigration, migration, history, science and technology, community building, peacemaking, sustainability, ethics, bioethics, ethnobiology, ecology, and more.

5

More Than Headlines
Preaching in Practice

Imagining and influencing more generative relationships in the world around us rely on us understanding interconnectedness. We do not experience life as "one thing at a time." Politics always involves what it means to be human and survive in the world. And what it means to be human always entails existing alongside the wider creation. We do not experience life in isolation from our neighbor, be that human or the natural world. We live interconnected lives. More life-sustaining futures depend on our willingness to give attention to the full spectrum of life as it takes shape in front of us.

Preaching that attends to the fullness of life requires both an awareness of our interconnectivity and our accountability to our neighbor in radical love practice. We bring awareness of this interconnectivity and accountability to our conversations about Scripture and the faith tradition. But most importantly, these conversations take place in community. These conversations feed the coffee hours, Bible studies, and sermons that impact how people of faith participate in the world around us.

In what follows, I will offer glimpses of the shape that sermon development and preaching may take. I keep in mind the obstacles we construct and our tendency toward surrender when engaging Scripture and life as well as addressing the big-picture subject matters and enduring questions from the previous chapters. But before moving forward with these possible routes for sermon development, I must say something about the pitfalls and possibilities we encounter when approaching preaching in this way.

Finite Imaginings

Bringing a deep awareness of life and its complexities to preaching is not about getting it right. Inevitably, we will miss the mark. And that's okay. Having the humility to recognize that, in preaching, we're grasping for something we never fully achieve is a call to integrity and accountability without a need for perfection. When we approach the preaching task with the assumption that we are "right" and that our message is ironclad, it may say more about the danger of our egos than the message itself. Perfection and integrity are not synonymous.

Admitting that the things we say and do in the name of faith are imperfect and incomplete brings a nimbleness and dexterity to preaching. For with it comes the need to reassess our claims in an ongoing manner as we listen with our hearts to the ground. Recognizing the finitude in our imaginings is precisely what brings preacher and community to the table to vet how their confessions of faith, claims about life, and actions in the world do or do not align.

Our recognition of limits in faith claims is what frees both preacher and community to take the risks most needed. Together they take the risk both in the name of the fatalities we have witnessed and in the name of possible futures we have yet to witness. This risk is one of informed discernment based on our best finite imaginings of the Spirit's love and hopes in the world today. The process will look different for every preacher and community, as it is contextual and temporal. But the intent of the process remains the same. We seek integrity and accountability to the entire creation in the claims we make. So we raise questions to lift the veil on the world, Scripture, and tradition in order to follow the paths of additional curiosities and inquiries as they arise. Preaching is calculated risk-taking,[1] as we do not know where these paths may lead.

Hoped-for Outcomes

The previous chapters offered core concerns and possibilities in conversation with major subjects that impact our lives day in and day out: fleshy parts, taboo conversations, and struggles for belonging. I've proposed enduring questions the community of faith and the preacher might ask of any given passage of Scripture or scenario in the world out of an awareness of these matters. As stated, enduring questions always make room for deeper and contextualized inquiry when engaging specific scenarios. Every juncture of informed discernment is guided by a concern for how what we profess can contribute either to the deterioration of life on the ground or to its transformation toward more just outcomes.

The preacher is concerned with honoring the totality of what it means to be human—*fleshy parts*. Part of honoring our humanity entails confronting anything that seeks to diminish the sanctity of life in body, mind, and spirit. With this in mind, the work of the preacher is to open a space for collective discernment, to act against the undue suffering of our neighbors, and to intervene in ways that support their ability to flourish and, at minimum, live. The sermon outcomes seek to spur earnest attention to recovering the sanctity of human life as an engaged practice of faith.

The preacher also gives attention to foregrounding collective accountability in addressing *taboo conversations*. Collective accountability includes how our social agreements, access to resources, and named values impact our basic needs and longings for connection. In the move toward greater accountability to neighbor and God in sermon development, the preacher seeks to name what is awry and thwarts more just ways of living together. Sermon outcomes rely on the veracity of lament as a precursor to repentance in spiritual and socially actionable ways.

And finally, the preacher remains mindful of those things that contribute to our further estrangement from one another and the wider creation, our *struggles for belonging*. Such things include an overemphasis on otherworldly rescue at the expense of stewardship here and now as well as the misguided human right to domination, be that the domination of people or aspects of creation. Sermon outcomes seek to foster greater connectedness and recognize our mutual dependence; they lay claim to God's desires for salvaging *all* of creation through radical love practice.

Preaching that maintains connections between honoring the sanctity of life, collective accountability, and mutual dependence creates the space for a community to imagine radical love practice in ongoing ways, even as the times change. In this way, the preacher and community express a willingness to name where we are still tied to hate and to seek the sustenance of life through love. And naming creates a space for the community to imagine what being rescued from the finality of death to life looks like today for the entire creation.

The process of naming and imagining opens the community to revelation. Namely, we are opened to the most creative and generative disclosures of what participating in the ongoing availability of a relationship with God entails here and now. This participation has concrete possibilities. The hoped-for outcome of preaching includes this openness to an ongoing participation in communion with all that's *holy*. It's a communion that involves continuity and care in relationship with *all* that neighbors us on this side of our residency in creation.

Glimpses of Informed Discernment

Preaching traditions hold within themselves a type of permissive will or options. These options honor the best parts of faith traditions, even as they challenge the most dangerous parts of that same tradition for better outcomes. The preacher discerns their way to these options.

For a glimpse into using such an awareness and process for preaching, I've paired each of our previous subjects with a passage of Scripture followed by a sermon excerpt. The pairings are random and do not signal a topical approach to preaching. They do not attend to any one specific problem in the world at hand. In other words, these are not single-issue or single-headline sermons. These are pieces that emerge out of an awareness of the multiple issues at hand in our world.

For example, you will not find a sermon here on sustainability and the environment, though one could preach that sermon. But you will find the thoughts of someone who is aware of creaturely beings and how the natural creation is integral to the world in which we live. And more importantly, I am convinced that we cannot ignore our mutual dependence on both our human neighbors and the created world.

Discerning the message of a sermon brings to light different concerns depending on the things going on around us, the concerns of the community, or the subjects for which our own hearts are most passionate. For instance, I've included a sermon I preached on Judges 11 following the November 2016 US presidential election. This sermon took a different shape and had different accent points than it would have had four months earlier.

Keep in mind that informed decision-making is deliberate decision-making. The best practices of preaching keep all major concerns in mind, even as the preacher makes choices about where the accent lies in a specific message. In other words, preachers seek to remain aware of what they are leaving behind or raising up in the choices they make.

Fleshy Parts

This exploration of Matthew 15:21–28 assumes the enduring questions of chapter 2 while naming new questions that may emerge when thinking alongside the particulars of both Scripture and the world at hand.

> Jesus left that place and went away to the district of Tyre
> and Sidon. Just then a Canaanite woman from that region
> came out and started shouting, "Have mercy on me, Lord,

Son of David; my daughter is tormented by a demon." But he did not answer her at all. And his disciples came and urged him, saying, "Send her away, for she keeps shouting after us." He answered, "I was sent only to the lost sheep of the house of Israel." But she came and knelt before him, saying, "Lord, help me." He answered, "It is not fair to take the children's food and throw it to the dogs." She said, "Yes, Lord, yet even the dogs eat the crumbs that fall from their masters' table." Then Jesus answered her, "Woman, great is your faith! Let it be done for you as you wish." And her daughter was healed instantly.

Just before this scene opens, Jesus has been in conversation with the religious leaders and teachers of the day about tensions between tradition, desires of God, faith, and how the status of one's heart impacts the capacity for faithful words and actions. One tradition of preaching this text focuses on Jesus, often tidying up his initial passive interaction with this woman and his likening her to a dog—all in the name of Jesus "trying to prove a point" for the sake of the disciples and others or even to teach this woman a great lesson of faith.

As with any text, multiple insights emerge through a close and immersive reading. Alternative interpretations may emerge as we immerse ourselves in the flesh-and-blood drama unfolding in the story. To help us seek new insights, we might ask questions of the text, including the following:

* What is the history of and the tensions between those named as the House of Israel and those of the region of Tyre and Sidon? The Canaanites?
* What similar tensions between groups in our world come to mind?

* What are the implications of the use of *dog* to refer to this woman and Gentiles? What equivalencies come to mind in history or in the present day?
* What can be said about demon possession in the historical content of this passage? Is possession mental, physical, or spiritual? How might the way we describe this possession be heard as stigmatizing any physical body in our contemporary world?
* How do we recover the bodies of this passage and those of our world and not deny that some bodies are not restored or healed? How do we avoid equating the lack of restoration to a deficit in their faith?
* When you consider the woman, where do you see her in the world today? Who is she?
* How did her status impact her ability to receive care for her daughter? Where was her community? What was the community's responsibility to her?
* Are there instances in which we would want to be leery of settling for "crumbs"? How might these crumbs be used as an excuse to continue practicing inequity?
* What would happen if we read this passage from a different "fleshy" point of view—that of the daughter? The disciples? Jesus? The onlookers?

The sermonic excerpt that follows offers *one* of many possible outcomes of exploring this passage while keeping in mind the joys and sorrows of being life-filled flesh.

Sermon Outcomes

I've preached a version of this sermon in both communities of faith and academic contexts with diverse demographics. When crafting a sermon for different contexts, I urge preachers to understand that the main message remains the same, although it is further refined as the context shifts. Giving attention to the distinctiveness of "fleshy" details across contexts builds the bridge to shared understanding.

In the sermon, my intent was to counter the ways in which we easily dismiss the significance and well-being of people in our world while drawing correlations to those dismissals in the text. Part of this work included humanizing the nameless Canaanite woman and her daughter as well as emphasizing the incarnational nature of the life of Jesus and his ministry. Reclaiming the viability of flesh in the ministry of Jesus, even in its fallibility, helped me work from within the tradition to claim the viability of the lives of the Canaanite woman and her daughter. In doing so, I hoped to reclaim the viability of the lives of their contemporaries in the present world.

For this sermon, I chose to name the unnamed woman Sharon. I gave her daughter the name Tina. And I told the story from the vantage point of a character never named in the story, Tina's aunt, Tasha. Tasha replaces the narrator of the text as she recounts the story of her sister to her niece and us, the current listeners of the narrative. For me, these choices support the important work of showing a full human being with a history, family, and community, even though she was unnamed. It amplifies the role of the Canaanite woman in the life and ministry of Jesus. The choices emphasize the role of women carrying on generational memories and teaching the faith, which is important to offset the male preferential of our sacred texts in the history of interpretative practices. Finally, I hoped it would reverberate outward to naming, recovering, and humanizing those we often diminish on a daily basis in present times.

"Great Is Your Faith"

. . . There is a difference between being willing to persistently seek God and being willing to struggle alongside God for what is most possible. Struggle takes a different type of effort. Struggle says, "I know God could intervene from the outside, but sometimes God just doesn't." But that's okay because there is a piece of God already residing in me. If I show up, God is showing up. Folks picked cotton and pulled tobacco, moaning, "Come down, Moses," as they struggled with God for the promises of God. Folks boycotted buses as they struggled alongside God for the promises of God. The depression doesn't leave, but you keep showing up every day. God didn't take the cancer away, but you still believe. The pain and disappointment haven't left, but you keep moving instead of giving up.

Sharon enters an exchange with Jesus for the manifestation of what she believes to be God's will and promise. And this exchange takes place right in the public square. It's personal, it's social, and it's political. I sense Sharon's willingness to enter the struggle in word and action pulling at Jesus's divinity, as their humanities touched in real time. The circumstances have been created for the truth to emerge right in their midst. Jesus's ministry is about to expand, and the vision of God will be realized, all because this woman was willing to struggle alongside Jesus.

We begin seeing the human and divine pulling at each other in Jesus. He can stick to his mission, or he can respond to the God in her that is tugging at the God in him. Jesus faces a quandary; he moves from "I ain't here for you" to "But it's not fair." Jesus's response is no longer an answer constrained to yes or no, but it is as if she is pulling him and he's compelled—summoned or called—to enter into this dialogue with her as Sharon speaks and moves in his presence.

Jesus says, "It is not fair to take the children's food and throw it to the dogs." We can't ignore it: Jesus has just likened this woman to a dog. Ouch! That had to sting! That had some bite! And Sharon had the nerve to respond and say yes—code for "True, yea, that's me!"

And as soon as I was up in arms at the undisputed yes, Tasha took me aside and said, "Don't get offended too much, Lisa. Because now what people really think about us is out in the open. We're considered dogs, pagans, unclean, unfit, not a part of the outright blessing of God." They say, "Oh, that's just those people." Something different happens when the power of the unspoken is removed. When people are truthful and honest about how they really feel, we can stop pretending like nothing is wrong.

Since it's actually been said, we can stop fighting problems that people claim don't exist. Before, instead of saying how they really felt aloud, they moved the public auction block of slavery to the silent auction of prison. They discarded and herded our bodies like livestock, claiming we just commit more crimes. Instead of saying how they really felt, they slowly built shops, restaurants, grocery stores, and housing they knew we couldn't afford—so eventually we had to move out of the neighborhood. Instead of saying, "You're not as good," they just pay me less, give me a different job title, and then call me a criminal when I think of inventive ways to survive. So Tasha says, "No, don't be put off by my sister's response, because now she has something to work with."

And as Jesus is turning on his heels to walk away, with a sigh of relief because he has spoken truth that cannot be negated, Sharon says, "Yet even the dogs eat the crumbs that fall from their master's table." She is yet again quick and brilliant.

The word used in verse 27 (*kunaria*) refers to a house dog as opposed to a wild dog that is out running through the streets. I hear Sharon essentially saying, "It is not about me being a dog; it's how my 'doggyness' is defined. I'm still a part of the household. And at minimum, I'm entitled to the crumbs that fall from the table inside the house." Jesus might remember Sharon in chapter 16 when he feeds the four thousand and picks up seven baskets of crumbs. Maybe he has recollections of the twelve baskets of crumbs he picked up after feeding the five thousand. The crumbs are the overflow of God's outright blessing.

She took the thing that had the potential to bite and sting and defined it for herself. Great is your faith. Sharon moves and stakes her claim even in the face of opposition. Believing that she, too, was included in the blessing of God, she enters a struggle and clarifies who she is and the bare minimum to which she's entitled: God's blessing. She helps clarify the vision of God for the entire land. Great is your faith. Participating in limited visions of who we are may very well limit the visions of God. Once we begin breaking open the box and raising holy hell on our street, we just might become participants in God's work and cosigners of God's vision. We can't afford to be silent anymore. We have to speak up and enter the struggle with God.

Taboo Conversations

This exploration of Judges 11:28–40 assumes the enduring questions of chapter 3 while naming new questions that may emerge when thinking alongside the particulars of both Scripture and the world at hand. Only segments of the full passage are offered here.

Then the spirit of the Lord came upon Jephthah, and he passed through Gilead and Manasseh. He passed on to Mizpah of Gilead, and from Mizpah of Gilead he passed on to the Ammonites. And Jephthah made a vow to the Lord, and said, "If you will give the Ammonites into my hand, then whoever comes out of the doors of my house to meet me, when I return victorious from the Ammonites, shall be the Lord's, to be offered up by me as a burnt offering." . . . Then Jephthah came to his home at Mizpah; and there was his daughter coming out to meet him with timbrels and with dancing. She was his only child; he had no son or daughter except her. When he saw her, he tore his clothes, and said, "Alas, my daughter! You have brought me very low; you have become the cause of great trouble to me. For I have opened my mouth to the Lord, and I cannot take back my vow." She said to him, "My father, if you have opened your mouth to the Lord, do to me according to what has gone out of your mouth, now that the Lord has given you

vengeance against your enemies, the Ammonites." . . .
So she departed, she and her companions, and bewailed
her virginity on the mountains. At the end of two
months, she returned to her father, who did with her
according to the vow he had made. She had never slept
with a man. So there arose an Israelite custom that for
four days every year the daughters of Israel would go out
to lament the daughter of Jephthah the Gileadite.

The plot of this text accelerates around a vow, subsequent reactions, and finally, the fate of the person the vow most impacts—the daughter of Jephthah (Bat-Jephthah). Bat-Jephthah is presumed to be sacrificed as a burnt offering in response to her father's vow to God. The story is constrained in showing the full dimensions of Bat-Jephthah beyond her being a commodity for exchange in familial, social, political, and religious structures. Though felt tensions around the scenario arise in some places of the text, by the end, no one makes an intervention that changes the fatal outcome—not even God. There seems to be enough blame to go around.

Often this text is preached in ways that remain within the same constraints that the plot itself operates. In the best of these instances, Jephthah remains the focus of the show, as the preacher calls listeners to avoid irresponsible vows before God that result from a lack of faith. But the sermon rarely extends to questioning the social pacts, laws, and named religious values in ways that reject the death of a person as "Just the way things are."

Beyond the enduring questions of chapter 3, more particular questions from an encounter with this text may include the following:

* What do we make of God's inferred leading in matters of war? And what will those choices infer about the connections between social pacts, God, people groups, and leaders in our present day?
* What are the connections between sexed talk, Bat-Jephthah's fate, and her value in the world of the text?
* How does one's value impact access to resources, safety, relationships, and outcomes in the text? In our world?
* What images, actions, and characters come to mind as you think of personal and shared responsibility in this story?
* Listen closely to the silences, noises, and dialogue in this passage. Who is participating in them, and what is happening in them?
* Where do you hope God is in this story? Where do you hope God isn't in this story, and why?
* What would be required for Bat-Jephthah to live? Test your theory by rewriting the story so she lives.

Sermon Outcomes

I preached the following sermon two weeks after the 2016 US presidential election at the Academy of Homiletics in San Antonio, Texas, for an opening worship service. This version of the sermon assumes listeners have some knowledge of the story, as it was a gathering of theological and religious educators who taught preaching. I've included this version of the sermon to demonstrate how we seek to illuminate a message and the core issues differently depending on the community before us, even as the basic pulse of a message and the core issues remain the same. Near the end of the sermon, you will be tuned in to how I would take the message in a different direction had I preached it in a worship service in a community of faith, which I have done.

"Holy Disturbances"

To find ourselves unsettled and our equilibriums shaken can be difficult and unnerving. And yet sometimes the most unsettling and disturbing factors are when chaos creeps in on us by the hands of someone else, for every force of action has an equal and opposite reaction. Living with the consequences of people casting lots for your very life can be difficult, to say the least. And these times are all the more bewildering when the forces that wield themselves on us can only be summed up as calculated foolishness or life doing its random drive-by. The chaos that invades our lives hurls through as our hearts are left scared, our bodies mangled and bruised, and our families are disbanded and displaced.

Life is often interrupted by events or circumstances that constrict our hoped-for future. New fences and walls are erected where they did not and need not exist. Our plans of going the entire stretch of the field are now confined and restrained to only a portion of the field by partitions and obstacles.

And yet there is nothing new under the sun in the history of our lives and times.

The same script but a different cast of characters.

So today, as we resist the way in which life and the world lull us into the erasure of history and the mis-memory of facts, we also resist the means by which our text seems to cajole or wants to conjure the hope of mismemory and the erasure of someone; she is only referenced as Jephthah's daughter, Bat-Jephthah. BJ is her name for tonight. Her life is interrupted and turned upside down by the hands of someone else.

BJ leaps from the door of her house with tambourines, laughter, singing, and dancing—just like her great-aunts. She leaps only to meet the disturbing facts of her new reality. Her life will be changed forever. BJ learns her father has bartered away her life. Her life! Not his life, but hers. At the brink of the battlefield, BJ's father, the lauded hero of the mismemory of our faith story, paused and petitioned God like a genie in a bottle. And now the violence he did upon his "enemies" in a trail of tears has come home to his doorstep and landed on an innocent bystander—BJ. It seems he's sacrificed her life for the greater good. Interesting that it wasn't his life he bartered away. It wasn't his job security, health insurance, or tenure. No, he unnecessarily bartered someone else's future under the claims of faith, actually grounded in the absence of faith. Disturbing realities.

But the response that follows in our holy writ is just as disturbing as the barter itself, and we haven't even arrived at the burning altar. When BJ's father delivers the news of his bad judgment, his response is one of displaced blame, outrage, and seeming dismay. BJ looks at him squarely and, without blinking an eye, says, "Do what you gotta do. Do what you already decided you had the power to do." A life has been bartered in the worst way, and there are two responses: shock versus "Oh, okay."

I am convinced BJ knows she lives in a world in which some are perpetual burnt offerings. This is the same world in which a woman is thrown out the door by her live-in abuser and raped all night long within an inch of her life. And when he finds her on the doorstep, he cuts her body into pieces and sends it out across the land (Judg 19). This is the same world in which women are described in terms of their sexual ripeness and in relationship to their husbands, brothers, fathers, and captors. This is the same world in which the people of God are claiming themselves as warriors and running around like the biblical Taliban while claiming their enemies are the terrorists. In this world, BJ's power, authority, and ability to speak are constantly snatched away by the looming threat of death. In this world, she lives as the "walking dead" every day—with or without a spoken vow or a ballot. This is the world in which the unspoken vows are laws of stop and frisk, death by blackness, violation by gender, deportation with or without documentation, and curse by pleasure. Bodies have been burning on the altar of this world far too long for "us"—I mean for BJ not to know.

BJ's father seemed shocked, but BJ says, "Okay." So she turns to say to the world that has marked her as disposable and dispensable, "And so it goes, as it has always gone. Life goes on. You be outraged, but I am going to do what I have always done—set the terms of my existence in a system that was never built for my survival, let alone my thriving."

Even when our very lives and livelihood are put on the auctioning block, we still have some decisions to make. And these are not decisions about acquiescing to calculated or unpredictable chaos. These are decisions about how we will live now in the world laid out before us.

BJ goes to the mountain with those she would recognize with or without the presence of a safety pin.[2] Well, I know them because they have held the line with me from the beginning. BJ and her partners in solidarity go to the mountain to claim the dignity of her life because they are utterly disturbed by a world that would claim otherwise. They begin doing the work on the mountain. The work that the world in which they lived refused to make room for. They name what should not be; they claim life as something that is not up for bartering, negotiating, or a vote.

The story is so familiar to us that we know how it ends. There are no surprises. BJ returns home from the mountain, and her body burns. It is a disturbing reality but not a surprise.

Now, at this point in the sermon, if we were sitting with the student of preaching or out in a community of faith, we would contend, "Oh preacher, now you must address the hard questions. You must ask the question begging to be asked and that we do not want to attend. If you do not attend to the question, you have done an injustice to your people and the text."

In ordinary circumstances, that question would involve calling God to the carpet. Holding court with God. And asking, "Where is God?" or "What's up, God?" But this is not the hard question for those of us trained to be Houdinis of the text and theological gymnasts; this is not the hard question. Often we don't have such a hard time questioning the location of God's presence in this room. We don't have issues with putting God on trial or calling God to task.

We have amazed students, congregations, and colleagues with the linchpin and hook of this text. We wind our way up to God's presence and disapproval of what is taking place. And we locate that disapproval in the wailing of the women who went to the mountain and whose daughters return to the mountain year after year. And whose daughters Jeremiah the weeping prophet calls in to wail with him. We are quite fine with the rationales of human free will, that sometimes God works from below, and that Red Seas aren't always parted. We are fine with the reminder that the last time God seemed to initiate a sacrifice close to this one, the boy Isaac was spared. There is no precedent of God requiring human sacrifice.

So "Where is God?" is not the hard question to a room of homileticians; we would do ourselves and the text an injustice to stop there.

No, for us, the hard questions are more akin to, Where was the priest when this was going down? Where are the teachers and interpreters of the law when people are gathering wood, newspapers, and lighter fluid for this burning that's about to happen on the altar? What did the teachers, the priests, and interpreters of the law leave undone that allowed for folk who knew better to be silenced by a rowdy mob marching bodies to an altar to be burned over and over again? They marched while touting perverted stories of faith, life with God, and life with one another. When the egos of human beings, eager to participate in God's kin-dom come, did things that disturbed the depths of our being, the priest and the teachers seemed to be absent.

You mean to tell me the priest did not offer to buy out the sacrifice of BJ? The interpreters of the law never said there was another way to handle it. Maybe they thought that the people who needed to hear it most would come to them behind iron gates and long hallways with whiteboards—as opposed to their going out there, where religion really happens.

Hard questions. Where was the community to tell BJ's father, "You are not recalling the full story. No, the free-moving and unconstrained spirit of God did not move based on your restrictions and dictation. God responded to the cries we sent up for deliverance from the occupation of the Ammonites. And because God didn't believe our word was bond, we put away our idols and began confessing our sins. And BJ's father, we just so happened to place your negotiating, looting, bartering self in leadership of the army"?

What if *we*, the priests, the teachers of the faith, and the interpreters of the law days, weeks, months, and years ago were to say, "No, wait! This entire fiasco is going down based on a lie"?

What we fail to understand is that the same system that wasn't built for BJ wasn't built for her father either. A system not built for the most vulnerable eventually hunts down everyone.

Where were the priests, interpreters, and teachers when babies were gunned down in the street, unnecessary betrayal and violence wreaked havoc upon lives, and hate speech consumed our everyday lives? The very same powers we protest being stowed away in the bedrooms of our homes began leaking from the cracks of our front doors and our offices.

What I appreciate about our text is that even when the priest and teachers did not show up, there was still some faith and common sense in the land. Others took to the streets and began marching. They wail year after year, as bodies are marched to the altar, year after year after year until someone recognizes that God is prompting their wailing. Year after year after year until enough people say, "You've gotten the story wrong." Year after year until someone says, "You are misremembering the faith. This ought not be so."

The weeping, wailing women make a decision to keep the line and create chaos, but it is unlike the chaos that espouses death. They cause people to be unnerved for the sake of what life should be. And their daughters keep the line. Their daughters' daughters keep the line. They beg us to remember that we have no other options than those that disrupt the status quo and declare life over death at every single turn.

We find no solace in this text. We only find a disturbance so deep that it evokes a holy memory. It is the memory that life should be so much more than this. As the people of God, we are to be so much more than this.

This is God's grace to us—the Spirit's willingness to keep begging and bidding questions to be asked:

Where were we?
Where will we go?

What will we do?

And with whom will we sit as priests, teachers, and interpreters of the faith?

What more shall I say about those who have gone before us in faith? I don't have time to tell you about Hagar, Shiphrah, Puah, Deborah, BJ, and the daughters of Israel. And all these, though they were not always commended for their faith and did not see the promise, they decided to make a little noise anyway for the entire creation of God. *Please, may it be so.*

Struggles for Belonging

This exploration of Genesis 16 and 21 assumes the enduring questions of chapter 4 while naming new questions that may emerge when thinking alongside the particulars of both Scripture and the world at hand. Only excerpts from the chapters are included below.

But Abram said to Sarai, "Your slave-girl is in your power; do to her as you please." Then Sarai dealt harshly with her, and she ran away from her. The angel of the Lord found her by a spring of water in the wilderness, the spring on the way to Shur. And he said, "Hagar, slave-girl of Sarai, where have you come from and where are you going?" She said, "I am running away from my mistress Sarai." The angel of the Lord said to her, "Return to your mistress, and submit to her." The angel of the Lord also said to her, "I will so greatly multiply your offspring that they cannot be counted for multitude." (Gen 16:6–10)

The child grew, and was weaned; and Abraham made a great feast on the day that Isaac was weaned. But Sarah saw the son of Hagar the Egyptian, whom she had borne to Abraham, playing with her son Isaac. So she said to Abraham, "Cast out this slave woman with her son; for the son of this slave woman shall not inherit along with my son Isaac." . . . But God said to Abraham, "Do not be distressed because of the boy and because of your slave woman. . . . As for the son of the slave woman, I will make a nation of him also, because he is your offspring." . . . And she departed, and wandered about in the wilderness of Beer-sheba. When the water in the skin was gone, she cast the child under one of the bushes. Then she went and sat down opposite him a good way off, about the distance of a bowshot; for she said, "Do not let me look on the death of the child." And as she sat opposite him, she lifted up her voice and wept. And God heard the voice of the boy; and the angel of God called to Hagar from heaven, and said to her, "What troubles you, Hagar? Do not be afraid; for God has heard the voice of the boy where he is." . . . Then God opened her eyes and she saw a well of water. She went, and filled the skin with water, and gave the boy a drink. God was with the boy, and he grew up; he lived in the wilderness, and became an expert with the bow. He lived in the wilderness of Paran; and his mother got a wife for him from the land of Egypt. (Gen 21:8–21)

The story names Hagar, Ishmael, Sarai, Abram, Isaac, the angel of the Lord, God, a well, the wilderness, and finally Ishmael's unnamed wife from the land of Egypt. It begins with continuing the thread of Sarai's barrenness and an unfulfilled promise of a son to Abraham and Sarai. In the midst of these circumstances, Sarai and Abram decide to use Sarai's slave girl, Hagar, to give birth to a future heir. Ishmael is born, but the conditions are untenable for Hagar. She runs away and returns at the words of the angel of the Lord, who meets her in the wilderness and gives her a promise. Isaac is born of Abraham and Sarah. This time, Hagar is put out into the wilderness, where God meets her and a well provides water for her and Ishmael. Ishmael grows up and lives in the wilderness, and Hagar, the former Egyptian slave girl, finds a wife for him from the land of Egypt. Her home.

Sermons on these texts give attention to the often recognized foreparents of the faith, Abraham and Sarah. The preacher might talk about Abraham and Sarah getting ahead of God's plans. Sarah is painted as the jealous villainess and Abraham as the go-along-to-get-along accomplice. When considering struggles for belonging, not in exclusion of the fleshy part or taboo conversations, the following questions might emerge from a close reading:

* What do we make of Hagar and her naming in relation to places and people?
* How do possession and violence connect to uprooting, a lack of home, and sustenance?
* What is the connection between Hagar and Sarai in their survival? What is the difference?
* What do we make of the angel of the Lord sending Hagar back to the place of Abram and Sarai?
* What is at risk in Hagar going back to the place of Abram and Sarai? What is at risk if she does not return?

* When we think of Hagar, Ishmael, Sarai, Abram, and Isaac, who do we think of today? What is at risk for them?
* What is the role of the wilderness and water in these two segments of the story?
* What happened between the last encounter at the well with God, Ishmael growing up, and Hagar finding him a wife from Egypt?
* What is the connection between Isaac and Ishmael and life continuing? Whose life?

Sermon Outcomes

The following is a sermon excerpt based on the narrative of these two chapters of Genesis that I've preached in congregational settings. Ordinarily, I would advise against preaching a sermon across the breadth of two chapters. These are decisions the preacher will need to discern when considering the dynamics of the world and text. I decided otherwise because of the dangers present in the first half of the story. The story describes Hagar's return to the place of her perpetrators at the direction of the angel of the Lord. Using both chapters is not the same as using both chapters to justify and leave unquestioned the ending of chapter 16.

My concern was the ways any interpretations that lacked nuance, in the name of God, could be used to promote death instead of our being rescued to life-sustaining possibilities in the present. Survivors of sexual and domestic violence were on my immediate radar. The message attends to the outcomes of considering others as someone's property while being removed from a sense of being in connection with others in a way that sustains and grounds us. This may be a snapshot of our human struggles for belonging.

"Torn between Bondage and Freedom"

I can almost see Hagar—stretched between reality and possibility. She gazes at Sarai. As she's washing the dishes, she sucks her teeth with a tsk. She moves about the streets. But every once in a while, the rhythm of her stride is interrupted by the stinging memory of someone laying hold of her body. Every once in a while, she feels the blood of her heart pulse through the cracks left behind by those long gone about their business. They did their dirt, and they left. For the rest of her life, Hagar has to live with the marks of someone else making plans for her. A line was crossed. Something happened.

Her world has been upended multiple times. We do not know what pushed her from her home. We do not know how she ended up with Sarai and Abram. She's now in search of a home away from her perpetrators—forced migration. She is looking for more than food and shelter. She is looking for the sustenance of protection and connection to space, land, and people. She's in search of a home but is not yet able to perceive it, even if her movement says, "More than this is possible."

By a spring of living water in the wilderness, she's met by a hologram of the Holy One. She's asked, "Where have you come from? Where are you going?" In other words, "Place yourself. Where do you belong?" Hagar could have responded in any number of ways:

"I'm going to Egypt."

"I am going to start a new life."

"I am on my way to be free—I'm from Egypt land."

"I left my master's house and am now on my way to build my own house."

But Hagar responds with, "I am running away from my mistress, Sarai." She is by a living spring. She is no longer in the household of her mistress, the place of bondage. When asked to name her orientation to space and place, she cannot answer the question being asked. "Place yourself, Hagar. Name your place, your direction, your future, and your past." Hagar's response amounts to "Bondage. Trauma. Forced pregnancy."

She is not to blame. All that has disoriented and uprooted her is to blame. She knows something more is possible but nevertheless lives in the mental and physical tensions between reality and future possibility. She's in the middle of placing herself anew, in the middle of belonging nowhere but somewhere, when this creekside chat turns disturbing.

The messenger of the Lord says what amounts to "Hagar, go back and live with, work with, and share space with the hands that harm you. Go back and take up residence with all that tried to serve up death to you. And I am sending you back with a promise of life, not death." The possibility of death and the promise of life now linger side by side.

I do not have an answer for this uncomfortable place in our text. But this is my commitment: we're going to wrestle and get more from God. We can't leave Hagar in the hands of her perpetrators. We can't leave her in the throes of bondage. But I don't have anything yet, so we're coming back to deal with God later.

Hagar goes back. Ishmael grows up. You know life goes on. But eventually, we find Hagar back in the wilderness. Her food has run out. Her water has run out. She's left the boy under a tree. And she is in a familiar place again—the wilderness—except this time, she didn't run away, so she can't sneak back in. There has been a permanent break from her house of terrors. Now she's facing another set of dilemmas she has never known. Suffering is familiar. To hope that something different is familiar. But to have that "something different begin to materialize" is a different ball game.

I can imagine that as she sits in this uncertain yet familiar place again in chapter 21, she may recall God's promise and the instructions to "go back." I'm sure she's distressed and at her wit's end, because the last time she was here, she was certain she saw God. So certain was she that she named God. She journaled about it so that she could remember it. So she would not forget. And I can hear her saying, "I distinctly remember God telling me to go to 'that place' and giving me 'a promise' before I went; I was even gifted by the living waters before I left."

We have to be careful not to conflate and confuse place, promise, and permanency. Place, promise, and permanency are not always connected. There are some real things at stake when we decide to break away and break off. Resources. Shelter. Food. Water. Rent money. Putting the kids through school. The stakes are high, and they are real. But that's okay. The place of provision and preparation is not the place of promise fulfilled. It is the place of planning. *Get a plan!*

In other words, we do not have to make a choice between surviving, our sanity, our safety, our health, our joy, and the promises of God. Promise goes along with you wherever you go. It zigzags around you in innocent joy and grows, just like Ishmael. And as a matter of fact, you have to survive in order for the promise to survive.

Although the house of Sarah and Abraham temporarily sheltered the promise of her and Ishmael's future, it was never intended to be the permanent solution. We know this because of the way the story ends; she is no longer the property of Sarah or Abraham. Look closer.

In chapter 21, every time Hagar is described or called, she is called by her name (except for her perps; they're always going to call her bound). She is no longer called the "Egyptian slave girl" or "Hagar, slave girl of Sarai." She is called "Hagar the Egyptian" or "Hagar." Her personhood is no longer associated with the systems, individuals, places, or labels that would attempt to keep her bound.

This time, when God shows up in the wilderness, God doesn't say, place yourself. God says, "I'm going to place, orient, and reorient you." The planning stage is over. It's game time.

When we're torn between bondage and freedom, life and death, God's grace is that thing that shows up with an intervention.

In verse 17, God says, "I heard the promise cry out. You might have lost all of your will to look for me again, and you may have lost all of your hope. But the promise is crying out, and not only am I the God who sees, but I'm also the God who hears." If you're crying, that means you still have some life left up in you.

As God calls Hagar, Hagar begins to respond to the instructions of God. The God who sees and hears begins to help Hagar see and envision anew. God gave her instructions and then opened her perception. Revelation happens right in that place—in the place between her bondage and her freedom, in the place between her demise and her renewal. It doesn't say that God created a well or the well miraculously appeared. On the contrary, it appears that the well was there all along; she simply needed a little reorientation to confirm that life wasn't over. The promise of life wasn't dead.

Hagar makes a way out of no way, right there in this "in-between and uncertain space." Piece by piece, brick by brick, one well after another well, one cup of water after another, in the wilderness, she and the promise take on new life.

We often think of the wilderness as a place of uncertainty, desolation, and instability. But this wilderness is different. She met God here, she received a promise here, and God meets her again right here. She and Ishmael find a place, a people, and relationships that do not kill them but sustain them.

God's desires are for us to live, to thrive—our whole self, flesh, spirit, and mind—here in this place.

"Hagar, What troubles you?"

Let's make life anew. *Amen.*

Conclusion
What Matters Most

Preaching the headlines isn't about preaching the headlines at all. It's about determining what matters most and why it matters, and then, proclaiming out of that conviction for the sake of living according to those convictions. Hoping against hope, these convictions entail believing that something of a more just world is desperately needed and possible.

A just world involves more right-fitting and unbroken relationships between all that dwells in creation, human and nonhuman. A just world affords a place in which the created integrity of all that dwells herein are honored without threat of extinction, avoidable suffering, and ongoing exile. A just world assumes our collective survival at minimum while creating a space for our collective sustenance and flourishing. A just world is a just creation.

Holy Priorities

People of faith care about a just creation because God cares about such a creation being at hand, here and now. The core of Christian faith traditions asserts that God responded out of love to the groans of creation, came to dwell among us, and lived out the most radical love practice. Life and life in its fullest form was the promise attached to that radical love practice, not life stolen, killed, and destroyed. If this is the case, it seems that perpetuating this promise is following the way of God—discipleship.

Anything that defies God's radical love practices is not love but insidious hate. Hate crucified and crucifies the holy incarnate. Hate allows and normalizes the destruction of life instead of its fullness. Hate is akin to the evil that destroys what is innocent. Wherever openings for hate exist, the powers and principalities that constantly turn us away from each other and God also exist. These openings define our sins—where we turn away from awareness of God and turn toward what actively devours both us and our neighbor. In these spaces, we claim neither love of neighbor nor love of God.

If the priority is sustaining life, we must confront where we have not sustained life, assume fewer answers and less certainty, ask better questions, and listen more to life on the ground. Preachers and religious leaders admit that the more they learn, the less they know, and they seek to better resource themselves for the work at hand. The everyday faithful commit to being more active and responsible in pursuing understandings of their faith and the world.

Together the entire community commits to opening a space that assumes less and interrogates more in order to discern paths to better futures. They ask genuine questions of the tradition and Scriptures, just as much as they interrogate the world. And they hold the claims made from Scripture and the tradition just as accountable to sustaining life as they do the world around us. All this work recognizes that our claims of faith can spur possibility and hope just as they can stir destruction and demise.

M. Shawn Copeland, in her book *Enfleshing Freedom*, offers that enfleshed freedom is spirit-filled flesh, being free to live, move, and achieve without constraint. And these places of such freedom in history and society are themselves sites of divine revelation. To this end, discipleship is embodied praxis. She states, "This praxis is the embodied realization of religious, cognitive, and moral conversion."[1] The evidence of discipleship is realized through our collective ability to be free literally—without the looming threat of premature death or erasure. So the question before Christian communities of faith is, "Where is our discipleship most evident, and where is it not?"

Greater Accountability

We must be clear about our priorities, which ultimately influence how we go about believing and doing in the world. People of faith do not believe in a vacuum, so our greatest responsibility lies in clinging to love of God and love of neighbor at all costs. If Christian communities do not more intentionally engage the world around us as an extension of faith, we are complicit in the ongoing injustice that takes place in the name of faith. Being clear about priorities also means being open to greater accountability in our failures.

Part of greater accountability within Christian communities of faith is being accountable beyond Christian communities of faith. This is about accountability to the collective well-being of creation. Such accountability recognizes the historical dangers that emerge when religion takes on power as its playmate. This accountability recognizes the visible veil of Christianity that enshrouds many of our interactions, policies, laws, and general social order in the United States and the Western world. Furthermore, it acknowledges the ways Christian "certainty" and "answers" have afforded some of the greatest transgressions against the fullness of life, in both our private and public lives. Some of the most unjust outcomes and violences in our midst have operated under a Christian veil, as they've relied on valuing life in terms of hierarchies and subordination.

Christian communities of faith perpetuating radical love practices in the world around us require multireligious conversation partners and collaborators. Indeed, we need the mirror of other faith traditions to hold us accountable to what lies at the core of our very own claims, as the robustness of these relationships reveals how we fail to pass our own standard of loving our neighbor. Practicing radical love also relies on moving beyond what we know to engage the sciences, lived wisdoms, policy experts, social workers, community organizers, and so much more. These practices require deep listening, honesty, truth telling, repentance, imagining, tearing down, and rebuilding. Preaching that supports such love practices relies on the very same things. Such preaching remains accountable to a community well beyond any given pew or sanctuary door, is collaborative at its core, and uses theological imagination for social reimagining.

Change and Faith

People often ask me, "If Christian traditions have created such demise and violence in history, why not leave them behind?

Why attend to them all?" For those outside the faith tradition, my most utilitarian response is, "The tradition still holds inherent power for so many people, and it sways our shared lives, whether Christian or not." For those within the faith tradition, my response points to the collective accountability we've discussed. Both responses assume we're trying to meet people where they are in order to usher in more life-bearing places for us all.

Many have difficulty coping with even minor, seemingly insignificant changes in their lives. Change can feel far more threatening when it addresses faith. This is partly because the beliefs and convictions that compose faith reside at the core of our identities.[2] We make sense of the world around us and of who we are based on what we've come to consider as our core values and fundamental beliefs. Faith is just as much about believing as it is about communal and family ties that, no matter how fractured or imperfect, provide a sense of belonging and security or at minimum create a felt loss of belonging and security.

I surmise that some of the deep resistance we experience when it comes to beliefs and change cloak fear. That fear resides somewhere along a continuum of "If I change my beliefs, I risk losing relationships—often significant relationships—on which I rely to function in the world, so if I change my beliefs, I lose my identity." In other words, sometimes people are not obstinate just to be difficult; instead, they fear losing something very tangible, even if they cannot articulate or recognize what that loss may be. Change feels risky. Change that involves faith feels even riskier; it is slow and difficult.

This type of shifting within communities of faith requires starting with the values and language people are familiar with for the sake of expanding them.[3] Sometimes this requires supplementing what they had with something more. We cannot leave people with less than what they had when they started. If we take something away, we must give them something in its stead. And not just anything but something that rings just as familiar and true as what we are asking them to lay aside. For instance, if we are asking a community to put down its practices of hate, we have to show both those practices for what they are and uplift a tradition that values practices of love. But even then, the work is still not finished; we continue to discern what those practices of love look like.

Community Not Harmony

When attending to the fullness of life, the risks we take in the pulpit parallel the risks we are asking of those in the pews, and those risks parallel the risks we are asking of the wider world. Considering these factors, effective proclaimers go beyond simply declaring, "We've got it all wrong, and we need to change," accurate though that may be. Instead, the work of preaching requires a sensitivity that brings people along, as opposed to attacking or coercing even if done in the name of what we feel is most true. There is an ethic in our preaching practices; they are both prophetic and pastoral. We are not just about having the right convictions; we are also about calling for change in ways that, whenever possible, enable communities to grow *together* in faith and toward maturity for a more just world.

Growing together in maturity as a community does not mean the absence of disagreement, tensions, outrages, or offense. In fact, it likely means experiencing more of all these things. Being in relationship is messy and hard, but it simultaneously presents delightful possibilities. Because we are complicated, life-filled, joyful, wounded, and mending beings, we will have to make decisions about when to hold back for the sake of bringing the community along. We also will have to make decisions about when we're obligated to proclaim what we hold as most true, despite the risks and potential negative consequences.

But to be clear, feeling uncomfortable or uneasy because we are challenged in our privileges and assumptions or because we disagree is not the same as being emotionally, physically, or spiritually threatened or unsafe. With this in mind, we also will need to make difficult decisions about when we can no longer be in community and must remove a festering wound from our midst that is causing harm and putting our collective best futures in jeopardy. At times, some of us will discern that it is we ourselves who must move on.

* * *

As stated in the beginning, the work before us is about resolutely claiming more with integrity. In all our discernment of text, tradition, and life on the ground, we keep the fullness of life, its sustainability, and its flourishing at the forefront. Life and its physical viability are viewed as uncompromisable, holy entities. In remaining accountable to the preservation of our neighbor's life, we remain accountable to God.

The community claims the conviction that God's just visions for the salvaging of life here and now are at hand and awaiting the participation of people of faith as they reveal themselves to *be the children of God.* This participation relies on the radical, moral, faith-filled, and generative aspects of imagination. Such imagination leads to concrete actions and relationships that testify to an awareness of God's ongoing revelation today. To be clear, these are not messages of gloom and doom. These are messages that conjure the most beautiful and holy things and even showcase where we witness the glimmers of God's appearance now. So whether its seeds are found in the headlines, at the dinner table, in the coffee shop, at school meetings, in the works of the artist or poet, in the public square, at the end of your road or street, or in the privacy of your own home—*pursue what matters most.*

NOTES

Chapter 1

1 Ronald J. Allen and O. Wesley Allen explore conversation as the work of preaching and expand David Tracy's framework of hermeneutics as conversation. Meaning making is the focus, and conversation privileges questions in the process of constructing meaning instead of determinations of what is true or false. Here, preaching foregrounds the goals of better understanding issues or topics, better understanding the perspectives of others, and finally supporting the ability of participants to better choose where to exist in relation to a topic. O. Wesley Allen and Ronald J. Allen, *The Sermon without End: A Conversational Approach to Preaching* (Nashville: Abingdon, 2015), 89–91.

2 Richard W. Voelz, using the foundations of critical pedagogy, offers a reframing of preaching as "preaching to teach," which destabilizes the dichotomies between pastoral and prophetic preaching. Preaching to teach seeks to inspire people, call them to a space of being active thinkers, and open up opportunities for them to consider transformative action in the world. Transformative action is that which literally transgresses the status quo. See Richard Voelz, *Preaching to Teach: Inspire People to Think and Act* (Nashville: Abingdon, 2019).

3 For more on agentive capacity in spaces of power differentials, see Saba Mahmood, "Agency, Performativity, and the Feminist Subject," in *Bodily Citations: Religion and Judith Butler*, ed. Ellen T. Armour and Susan M. St. Ville (New York: Columbia University Press, 2006), 177–225.

4 Harriet Washington uses this term instead of *food deserts*, which are regions that have limited access to affordable healthy food for their residents and are saturated with cheap, sugary, processed, fatty, and unhealthy food options; see Harriet A. Washington, "Keynote Address" (lecture, Public Theology and Racial Justice Medical Apartheid Conference, 2020), https://vimeo.com/445019683.

5 For a fuller treatment of the realm of God, see Brian K. Blount, *Go Preach! Mark's Kingdom Message and the Black Church Today* (Maryknoll, NY: Orbis, 1998).

6 Evelyn L. Parker, *Trouble Don't Last Always: Emancipatory Hope among African American Adolescents* (Cleveland, OH: Pilgrim, 2003), 11.

7 Parker, 11.

8 In other places, I have offered a more detailed account of interpreting Scripture for preaching while attending to the most vulnerable lived experiences; see Lisa L. Thompson, "Recovering Sacred Texts for Preaching," chap. 4 in *Ingenuity: Preaching as an Outsider* (Nashville: Abingdon, 2018).

9 Collaborative models for preaching encourage moving beyond an isolated process for sermon development. This movement makes a consideration for more lived experiences and an accountability to those lived experiences while decreasing the distance among preacher, the community, the world around us, and final interpretations. See Lucy Atkinson Rose, *Sharing the Word: Preaching in the Roundtable Church* (Louisville, KY: Westminster John Knox, 1997); John S. McClure, *The Roundtable Pulpit: Where Leadership and Preaching Meet* (Nashville: Abingdon, 1995); and Allen and Allen, *Sermon without End.*

10 John McClure argues for a framework of communication and its ethics through liturgical practices that open space for change. The community is to claim a type of "epistemic humility." Such humility is not bound to an enduring nature of the words or claims in preaching. But instead, we are loosened from being beholden to our claims in perpetuity as we admit the limits of our knowledge. The preacher and community admit these limits and open space for an ongoing

interrogation of the sincerity and insincerity of their claim. To this end, the community is not bound to words per se but bound to its faithfulness to a confession of faith and the commitments that accompany such a confession. This means a community and preacher possess an openness to interrogating how their words and actions may change and evolve in light of faith claims that profess love and justice before God and neighbor. See John S. McClure, *Speaking Together and with God: Liturgy and Communicative Ethics* (Lanham, MD: Lexington / Fortress Academic, 2018).

11 I've attended to this as a method for preaching against harmful texts while acknowledging the authority Scripture holds within communities of faith. See Thompson, "Recovering Sacred Texts."

12 For my fuller description of sacred storytelling and its relationship to formulating preaching claims, see Thompson, "Finding a 'Word from the Lord' for Today" and "Locating God and Faith on the Ground," chaps. 5 and 6 in *Ingenuity*, 107–72.

13 See Thompson, *Ingenuity*, esp. chap. 3, "Mining Life for Preaching," 37–62; and Cleophus James LaRue, *I Believe I'll Testify: The Art of African American Preaching* (Louisville, KY: Westminster John Knox, 2011), 59–60, 72–73.

14 See John S. McClure, *Mashup Religion: Pop Music and Theological Invention* (Waco, TX: Baylor University Press, 2011), esp. chap. 3, "Sampling, Remixing, and Mashup: Inventing the Theologically Possible."

15 I'm using the word *imagination* here as a gateway to accessing a moral imaginary that is practical and situated but never definitive about, sure of, or closed off to the hopes or outcomes of justice in the community and world; see Kelly Brown Douglas, "White Supremacy and the Legacy of Faith," Antoinette Brown Lectures, Vanderbilt University Divinity School, Nashville, TN, September 10, 2020; and Kenneth MacKendrick, "The Moral Imaginary of Discourse Ethics," *Critical Horizons* 1, no. 2 (February 19, 2010): 247–69.

16 For full models of collaborative preaching, see Rose, *Sharing the Word*; McClure, *Roundtable Pulpit*; and Allen and Allen, *Sermon without End*.

Chapter 2

1 For a fuller conversation about differentiations between the language of body and flesh when attending to the way we experience the world and the connection between Christian theological histories and social histories in tracing these connections, see Mayra Rivera, *Poetics of the Flesh* (Durham, NC: Duke University Press, 2015).

2 "'Home Truth' Shows a Mother's Fight for Justice after Husband Kills 3 Daughters," NBC News, October 3, 2018, https://www.nbcnews .com/news/latino/home-truth-shows-mother-s-fight-justice-after -her-husband-n915981.

3 "Chibok: The Village That Lost Its Daughters to Boko Haram," *Guardian*, May 15, 2014, https://www.theguardian.com/world/2014/may/ 15/chibok-nigeria-200-kidnapped-schoolgirls-boko-haram.

4 "About," Black Lives Matter, accessed March 1, 2019, https:// blacklivesmatter.com/about/.

5 "Get to Know Us," Me Too, accessed March 1, 2019, https://metoomvmt .org/get-to-know-us/.

6 "About #SayHerName," African American Policy Forum, accessed March 1, 2019, https://aapf.org/sayhername.

7 There is a documented history of people groups being viewed by others as being "partially" human or subintellectual or as not having souls and connections to a life force. These views make way for justifying their mistreatment and dehumanization across time, as they create hierarchies within humanity and the engagement of bodies in ways that serve the process and needs of commodification. See Phillis Sheppard, *Self, Culture, and Others in Womanist Practical Theology* (New York: Palgrave Macmillan, 2011); Eboni Marshall Turman, *Toward a Womanist Ethic of Incarnation: Black Bodies, the Black Church, and the Council of Chalcedon* (New York: Palgrave Macmillan, 2013); and Harriet Washington, *Medical Apartheid: The Dark History of Medical Experimentation on Black Americans from Colonial Times to the Present* (New York: Harlem Moon, 2006).

8 Emilie M. Townes explains that supporting the ability of faith leaders to lead communities out of a theological ethic of justice is not about

exhausting a list of things we often try to name when calling out injustices in the world, primarily because such a list is always incomplete. But instead, theological education committed to justice fosters a disposition and way of thinking that recognizes the presence of injustice. Emilie M. Townes, "An Overview of the Divinity School," Vanderbilt University board of trustees presentation, November 7, 2019, Nashville, TN.

9 Mayra Rivera describes the flesh as being more than body; it entails our living experience and participation in all the matter of the world around us. It takes on the social realities of our world as it is impacted by and impacts our social dimensions. *Flesh* has had different interpretations in history both inside and outside of religious traditions, all of which impact our current understandings of what it means to live as bodily beings. See Rivera, *Poetics of the Flesh*.

10 Nancy Lynne Westfield, womanist and scholar of religious education, describes evil as anything that distracts us from God. She underscores that the opposite of love is not death; the opposite of love is hate, which is the antithesis of a loving God. She explains that evil is anything that destroys or violates that which is innocent. Conversation with Nancy Lynne Westfield, May 2020.

11 The history of Platonized and Eurocentric Christianity theologies exasperate this dueling relationship of spirit and flesh; their permutation in the lives of racial-ethnic and gendered minorities complicates its deadly presence in our world. See Kelly Brown Douglas, *What's Faith Got to Do with It? Black Bodies / Christian Souls* (Maryknoll, NY: Orbis, 2005); Tamura A. Lomax, "#BlackSkinWhiteSin: From Pernicious Editing to Audacious Rescripting (Benediction)," Feminist Wire, accessed October 30, 2019, https://thefeministwire.com/2017/02/blackskinwhitesin-from-pernicious-editing-to-audacious-rescripting-benediction/; and Tamura A. Lomax, *Jezebel Unhinged: Loosing the Black Female Body in Religion and Culture* (London: Duke University Press, 2018).

12 Shelly Rambo, *Resurrecting Wounds: Living in the Afterlife of Trauma* (Waco, TX: Baylor University Press, 2017).

13 Rambo, 7.

14 Rambo, 7–10.

15 Rambo, 7–10.

Chapter 3

1 "Supreme Court Says Federal Law Protects LGBTQ Workers from Discrimination," CNN, June 15, 2020, https://www.cnn.com/2020/06/15/politics/supreme-court-lgbtq-employment-case/index.html.

2 Civil Rights Act of 1964, Pub. L. No. 88-352, 78 Stat. 241 (1964), enacted July 2, 1964, accessed April 18, 2021, https://www.govinfo.gov/content/pkg/STATUTE-78/pdf/STATUTE-78-Pg241.pdf.

3 "Civil Rights Act: How South Responds," *New York Times*, July 12, 1964, https://www.nytimes.com/1964/07/12/archives/civil-rights-act-how-south-responds.html.

4 "The Constitution: Amendments 11–27," Archives.gov, accessed August 30, 2020, https://www.archives.gov/founding-docs/amendments-11-27.

5 This is not a direct headline but a summation of multiple headlines around a 2018 Supreme Court decision for a case between a Colorado bakery owner and a same-sex couple requesting a cake for their wedding ceremony. Masterpiece Bakeshop, Ltd., et al. v. Colorado Civil Rights Commission et al., No. 16-111, decided June 4, 2018, https://www.supremecourt.gov/opinions/17pdf/16-111_new2_22p3.pdf.

6 "The Christian Right Has a New Strategy on Gay Marriage," Five-ThirtyEight, December 5, 2017, https://fivethirtyeight.com/features/the-christian-right-has-a-new-strategy-on-gay-marriage/.

7 "Transgender Health Protections Reversed by Trump Administration," NPR, June 12, 2020, https://www.npr.org/sections/health-shots/2020/06/12/868073068/transgender-health-protections-reversed-by-trump-administration.

8 Political action was taken on Muslim women's religious expressions in public as they moved about daily life. Ironically, during the pandemic

in 2020, all French citizens were mandated to wear face coverings. The questions on the table were why the initial ban was important in the first place, which power structures were in place that permitted the ban, who benefited the most from the ban, and what made it okay to mandate face coverings for all citizens. In some sense, the bodies of Muslim women, how they were adorned, and therefore how they were interpreted made way for legalizing discriminatory actions against them. The religious practices of these women then became bartered and negotiated at the hands of those most powerful to do so. "France Will Still Ban Islamic Face Coverings Even after Making Masks Mandatory," CBS News, May 12, 2020, https://www.cbsnews.com/news/france-burqa-ban-islamic-face-coverings-masks-mandatory/. See also "From Niqab to N95," NPR, May 27, 2020, https://www.npr.org/2020/04/28/847433454/from-niqab-to-n95.

9 For texts explicitly concerned with preaching, politics, and strategies, see Leah Schade, *Preaching in the Purple Zone: Ministry in the Red-Blue Divide* (Lanham, MD: Rowman & Littlefield, 2019); and O. Wesley Allen, *Preaching in the Era of Trump* (St. Louis: Chalice, 2017).

10 The most rigid expressions of our faith that become mechanisms of judgment, punishment, and harm are connected to power. But they are also dangerous offshoots of our attempts to ensure a connection to God. However, ensuring and regulating our connection to God and amplifying our awareness of God's presence are not the same. Nancy Lynne Westfield explains that the connection to the Holy is continual, as continual as the breath that sustains us. Practices of faith such as prayer, gathering, meditation, and even other ritualized engaged actions remind us of our connection to the Holy in our ongoing states of fragility and uncertainty. Conversation with Nancy Lynne Westfield, May 2020.

11 Christine Smith, ed., *Preaching as Weeping Confession and Resistance* (Louisville, KY: Westminster John Knox, 1992).

12 Luke Powery describes the presence of the Holy Spirit as the one who enables the preacher to lift both the joys and sorrows of the community

during the preaching moment. To this end, lament is the work made possible by the Spirit and has particular concerns and structures; see Luke Powery, "The Spirit of Lament and Celebration," in *Spirit Speech: Lament and Celebration in Preaching* (Nashville: Abingdon, 2009), 21–35.

13 Smith, *Preaching as Weeping*.

14 Practice theorist Pierre Bourdieu describes the tensions among power within systems, acknowledgment, and change. The practice of silencing and the illusion of all that surrounds us "just being the way it is" afford a lack of interrogation. Once something is named, there is the possibility of assumptions and invisibility being disrupted as they rise to the level of engagement. Essentially, naming moves power's background operations to the foreground; see Pierre Bourdieu, *Outline of a Theory of Practice*, Cambridge Studies in Social Anthropology 16 (Cambridge: Cambridge University Press, 1977), 170–71.

Chapter 4

1 Ecologist and ethnobotanist Gary P. Nabhan calls for a need for the restoryation of our relationship to the natural world and in the process of restoring the natural world. This means learning to narrate the relationships to the wider creation in broader and more holistic ways that do not center on the ego, dominion, and the needs of the people at the expense of a mutually sustaining relationship. Furthermore, this requires understanding that our relationship to place is connected to spiritual practices and the creation of stories of the past and present; see "Biocultural Restoration of Sacred Sites, Earth Day, and Restoration Ecology's Patron Saint," Gary Nabhan, March 8, 2020, https://www.garynabhan.com/news/2020/03/biocultural-restoration-of-sacred-sites-earth-day-and-restoration-ecologys-patron-saint/; and Robin Wall Kimmerer, *Braiding Sweetgrass: Indigenous Wisdom, Scientific Knowledge, and the Teaching of Plants* (Minneapolis: Milkweed Editions, 2013), 8–9.

2 "Stand with Standing Rock: Protect Protesters' Rights," ACLU, accessed June 1, 2020, https://www.aclu.org/issues/free-speech/rights -protesters/stand-standing-rock.

3 "Blood Diamonds," *Time*, accessed June 1, 2020, https://time.com/ blood-diamonds/.

4 "Temperatures in an Arctic Siberian Town Hit 100 Degrees, a New High," CNN, June 22, 2020, https://www.cnn.com/2020/06/22/ weather/siberia-arctic-100-degrees-climate-change-trnd/index.html.

5 Robin Wall Kimmerer places Indigenous ways of knowing in conversation with ecobiology to help reframe our relationship to creation and our understandings of it. She offers the passing down of stories, rituals, and ceremonies from generation to generation within Indigenous cultures as a way to understand an animate language, grammar, story, and sense of being of aspects of the natural world; these beings are much older than humanity and gift humans with sustenance but are not possessed by humanity. Ideas of relationships with creation are the emphasis here, not being in exile or estranged from creation. Attempts of owning, subduing, or conquering creation are continuous with storying our relationship to creation through exile and estrangement, which are themes in Christianity's storying of its relationship to the wider creation. See Kimmerer, *Braiding Sweetgrass*, 3–10, 48–59.

6 While there is inertia within the violence of these systems, that does not prevent an opportunity for a different type of space opening. Ted Smith describes the possibility akin to a space of negation breaking open, which is an alternative space of judgment that the violence and atrocities at hand cannot continue into the future. See Ted A. Smith, *Weird John Brown: Divine Violence and the Limits of Ethics* (Stanford, CA: Stanford University Press, 2015), esp. the conclusion.

7 For resources on the relationships between ecotheology, ecofeminisms, ecowomanism, and preaching, see Melanie L. Harris, *Ecowomanism: African American Women and Earth-Honoring Faiths* (Maryknoll, NY: Orbis, 2017); and Leah D. Schade, "Ecofeminist Theology and

Implications for Preaching," in *Creation-Crisis Preaching: Ecology, Theology, and the Pulpit* (St. Louis: Chalice, 2015), 92–116.

8 See Kimmerer, *Braiding Sweetgrass*, 22–32.

9 I do not ignore that there are various practices of holy communion across the Christian tradition and that some of those practices have been used in very exclusionary ways to bar participation in the ritual. This discussion is one that explores the openings, wherever they may be, within the claims of a community to expand those understandings for attending to engaged practices of faith.

10 This reproduction of a memory, a history, or a ritual for the sake of remembering is often described as a connection between mimesis and anamnesis.

11 The heaviness of participating in the memory in an unworthy manner is narrated with some of the greatest gravity in 1 Cor 11. Participants are called to remember lifesaving, rescuing, and sustaining activities and to live in awareness of those practices in order to avoid the judgments of weakness, illness, and death; see 1 Cor 11:17–34, esp. vv. 31–32.

12 *Anamnesis* is often used to describe the role of memory in Christian ritual and tradition. Toni Morrison—giving consideration to power, culture, and history—uses the term *rememory*. She describes this process as assembling or recovering memories of people, groups, and a culture whose histories are not fully known as they are recorded by the dominant chroniclers of history as objects and not subjects of history. *Rememory* becomes the thin veil between history, remembering, constructing, and forgetting; see Toni Morrison, "Rememory," in *The Source of Self-Regard: Select Essays, Speeches, and Meditations* (New York: Alfred A. Knopf, 2019).

13 Christopher D. Tirres argues for the role of ritual as a form of education, similar to the ways in which Richard Voelz reframes preaching as teaching: through lenses of critical and liberationist pedagogy. Both ritual and preaching have the opportunity to open space for transformative action within and by the community; see Christopher D. Tirres, "Embodied Faith in Action: Religious Ritual as

Reconstructive Education," in *The Aesthetics and Ethics of Faith: A Dialogue between Liberationist and Pragmatic Thought* (New York: Oxford University Press, 2014), 156–94; and Voelz, *Preaching to Teach.*

Chapter 5

1 Thompson, "Conclusion: Risk-Taking for the Sake of Life," in *Ingenuity*, 174–76.
2 After the 2016 elections, which solidified Donald J. Trump as president of the United States, some people wore safety pins as signs to others that they were allies, "safe" to encounter, and not affiliated with the perception of bigotry and prejudices that marked his campaign strategy and voter base.

Conclusion

1 See M. Shawn Copeland, *Enfleshing Freedom: Body, Race, and Being* (Minneapolis: Fortress, 2010), 127.
2 For more on faith and everyday practices see Miroslav Volf and Dorothy C. Bass, eds., *Practicing Theology: Beliefs and Practices in Christian Life* (Grand Rapids, MI: Eerdmans, 2002).
3 See Thompson, "Using the Familiar to Expand the Familiar," in *Ingenuity*, 61–64.

SELECT BIBLIOGRAPHY

Allen, O. Wesley, and Ronald J. Allen. *The Sermon without End: A Conversational Approach to Preaching*. Nashville: Abingdon, 2015.

Armour, Ellen T. *Signs and Wonders: Theology after Modernity*. New York: Columbia University Press, 2016.

Azaransky, Sarah, ed. *Religion and Politics in America's Borderlands*. Lanham, MD: Lexington, 2013.

Beasley, Vanessa B. "Presidential Rhetoric and Immigration: Balancing Tensions between Hope and Fear." In *Who Belongs in America? Presidents, Rhetoric, and Immigration*, edited by Vanessa B. Beasley, 1–18. College Station: Texas A&M University Press, 2006.

Black, Kathy. *A Healing Homiletic: Preaching and Disability*. Nashville: Abingdon, 1996.

Bowler, Kate, and Wen Reagan. "Bigger, Better, Louder: The Prosperity Gospel's Impact on Contemporary Christian Worship." *Religion and American Culture: A Journal of Interpretation* 24, no. 2 (Summer 2014): 186–230.

Campbell, Charles L. *The Word before the Powers: An Ethic of Preaching*. Louisville, KY: Westminster John Knox, 2002.

Carter, J. Kameron. *Race: A Theological Account*. New York: Oxford University Press, 2008.

Carvalhaes, Cláudio, ed. *Liturgy in Postcolonial Perspectives: Only One Is Holy*. New York: Palgrave Macmillan, 2015.

———. *What's Worship Got to Do with It? Interpreting Life Liturgically*. Eugene, OR: Cascade, 2018.

Cheng, Patrick S. *Rainbow Theology: Bridging Race, Sexuality, and Spirit.* New York: Seabury, 2013.

Choi, Jin Young. *Postcolonial Discipleship of Embodiment: An Asian and Asian American Feminist Reading of the Gospel of Mark.* New York: Palgrave Macmillan, 2015.

Coleman, Monica A. *Making a Way Out of No Way: A Womanist Theology.* Minneapolis: Fortress, 2008.

Cone, James H. *The Cross and the Lynching Tree.* Maryknoll, NY: Orbis, 2011.

Crawley, Ashon T. *Blackpentecostal Breath: The Aesthetics of Possibility.* New York: Fordham University Press, 2017.

Dahill, Lisa E., and James B. Martin-Schramm, eds. *Eco-reformation: Grace and Hope for a Planet in Peril.* Eugene, OR: Cascade, 2016.

Davis, Ellen F. *Getting Involved with God: Rediscovering the Old Testament.* Cambridge, MA: Cowley, 2001.

Day, Keri. *Religious Resistance to Neoliberalism: Womanist and Black Feminist Perspectives.* New York: Palgrave Macmillan, 2016.

De La Torre, Miguel A. *The Politics of Jesús: A Hispanic Political Theology.* Lanham, MD: Rowman & Littlefield, 2015.

Delgado, Teresa. *A Puerto Rican Decolonial Theology: Prophesy Freedom.* New York: Palgrave Macmillan, 2017.

Douglas, Kelly Brown. *The Black Christ.* Maryknoll, NY: Orbis, 1993.

————. *Stand Your Ground: Black Bodies and the Justice of God.* Maryknoll, NY: Orbis, 2015.

————. *What's Faith Got to Do with It? Black Bodies / Christian Souls.* Maryknoll, NY: Orbis, 2005.

————. "White Supremacy and the Legacy of Faith." Antoinette Brown Lectures, Vanderbilt University Divinity School, Nashville, TN, September 10, 2020.

Ellison, Marvin Mahan. *Making Love Just: Sexual Ethics for Perplexing Times.* Minneapolis: Fortress, 2012.

Florence, Anna Carter. *Preaching as Testimony.* Louisville, KY: Westminster John Knox, 2007.

———. *Rehearsing Scripture: Discovering God's Word in Community.* Grand Rapids, MI: Eerdmans, 2018.

Francis, Leah Gunning. *Ferguson and Faith: Sparking Leadership and Awakening Community.* St. Louis: Chalice, 2015.

Gafney, Wilda. *Womanist Midrash: A Reintroduction to the Women of the Torah and the Throne.* Louisville, KY: Westminster John Knox, 2017.

Gilbert, Kenyatta R. *Exodus Preaching: Crafting Sermons about Justice and Hope.* Nashville: Abingdon, 2018.

———. *A Pursued Justice: Black Preaching from the Great Migration to Civil Rights.* Waco, TX: Baylor University Press, 2016.

Grant, Jacquelyn. *White Women's Christ and Black Women's Jesus: Feminist Christology and Womanist Response.* Atlanta: Scholars, 1989.

Griffith, R. Marie. *Moral Combat: How Sex Divided American Christians and Fractured American Politics.* New York: Basic, 2017.

Harris, Melanie L. *Ecowomanism: African American Women and Earth-Honoring Faiths.* Maryknoll, NY: Orbis, 2017.

Harvey, Jennifer. *Dear White Christians: For Those Still Longing for Racial Reconciliation.* Grand Rapids, MI: Eerdmans, 2014.

Hill Collins, Patricia. *Black Feminist Thought: Knowledge, Consciousness, and the Politics of Empowerment.* New York: Routledge, 2000.

Hurd, Elizabeth Shakman. *Beyond Religious Freedom: The New Global Politics of Religion.* Princeton, NJ: Princeton University Press, 2015.

Jenkins, Willis. "Doing Theological Ethics with Incompetent Christians: Social Problems and Religious Creativity." In *Lived Theology: New Perspectives on Method, Style, and Pedagogy,* edited by Charles Marsh, Peter Slade, and Sarah Azaransky, 54–66. New York: Oxford University Press, 2017.

Jennings, Willie James. *The Christian Imagination: Theology and the Origins of Race.* New Haven, CT: Yale University Press, 2010.

Jones, Robert P. *White Too Long: The Legacy of White Supremacy in American Christianity.* New York: Simon & Schuster, 2020.

Kao, Grace, ed. *Asian American Christian Ethics: Voices, Methods, Issues.* Waco, TX: Baylor University Press, 2015.

Keller, Catherine. *Political Theology of the Earth: Our Planetary Emergency and the Struggle for a New Public*. New York: Columbia University Press, 2018.

Kim, Eunjoo Mary. *Preaching in an Age of Globalization*. Louisville, KY: Westminster John Knox, 2010.

Kimmerer, Robin Wall. *Braiding Sweetgrass: Indigenous Wisdom, Scientific Knowledge, and the Teaching of Plants*. Minneapolis: Milkweed Editions, 2013.

Lightsey, Pamela R. *Our Lives Matter: A Womanist Queer Theology*. Eugene, OR: Pickwick, 2015.

Lischer, Richard. *The End of Words: The Language of Reconciliation in a Culture of Violence*. Grand Rapids, MI: Eerdmans, 2005.

Lomax, Tamura A. "#BlackSkinWhiteSin: From Pernicious Editing to Audacious Rescripting (Benediction)." Feminist Wire. Accessed October 30, 2019. https://thefeministwire.com/2017/02/blackskinwhitesin-from-pernicious-editing-to-audacious-rescripting-benediction/.

———. *Jezebel Unhinged: Loosing the Black Female Body in Religion and Culture*. London: Duke University Press, 2018.

Machado, Daisy L., Bryan S. Turner, and Trygve Wyller, eds. *Borderland Religion: Ambiguous Practices of Difference, Hope, and Beyond*. New York: Routledge, 2018.

McBride, Jennifer M. *Radical Discipleship: A Liturgical Politics of the Gospel*. Minneapolis: Fortress, 2017.

McClure, John S. *Speaking Together and with God: Liturgy and Communicative Ethics*. Lanham, MD: Lexington / Fortress Academic, 2018.

McClure, John S., and Nancy J. Ramsay, eds. *Telling the Truth: Preaching about Sexual and Domestic Violence*. Cleveland, OH: United Church, 1998.

McCullough, Amy P. *Her Preaching Body: Conversations about Identity, Agency, and Embodiment among Contemporary Female Preachers*. Eugene, OR: Cascade, 2018.

Moss, Jada L. "The Forgotten Victims of Missing White Woman Syndrome: An Examination of Legal Measures That Contribute to the

Lack of Search and Recovery of Missing Black Girls and Women Notes." *William & Mary Journal of Race, Gender, and Social Justice* 25, no. 3 (2019): 737–64.

Moultrie, Monique Nicole. *Passionate and Pious: Religious Media and Black Women's Sexuality.* Durham, NC: Duke University Press, 2017.

Mount Shoop, Marcia W. *Let the Bones Dance: Embodiment and the Body of Christ.* Louisville, KY: Westminster John Knox, 2010.

Mumford, Debra J. *Exploring Prosperity Preaching: Biblical Health, Wealth, & Wisdom.* Valley Forge, PA: Judson, 2012.

Myers, Jacob D. *Preaching Must Die! Troubling Homiletical Theology.* Minneapolis: Fortress, 2017.

Phillips, Nichole Renée. *Patriotism Black and White: The Color of American Exceptionalism.* Waco, TX: Baylor University Press, 2018.

Powery, Luke A. *Spirit Speech: Lament and Celebration in Preaching.* Nashville: Abingdon, 2009.

Rambo, Shelly. *Resurrecting Wounds: Living in the Afterlife of Trauma.* Waco, TX: Baylor University Press, 2017.

Rieger, Joerg. *No Rising Tide: Theology, Economics, and the Future.* Minneapolis: Fortress, 2009.

Rivera, Mayra. *Poetics of the Flesh.* Durham, NC: Duke University Press, 2015.

Schade, Leah D. "Ecofeminist Theology and Implications for Preaching." In *Creation-Crisis Preaching: Ecology, Theology, and the Pulpit,* 92–116. St. Louis: Chalice, 2015.

———. *Preaching in the Purple Zone: Ministry in the Red-Blue Divide.* Lanham, MD: Rowman & Littlefield, 2019.

Sharpe, Melinda McGarrah. *Creating Resistance: Pastoral Care in a Postcolonial World.* Leiden, The Netherlands: Brill, 2019.

Sheppard, Phillis Isabella. "A Dark Body of Goodness Created in the Image of God: Navigating Sexuality, Race, and Gender, Alone and Together." In *Self, Culture, and Others in Womanist Practical Theology,* 143–72. New York: Palgrave Macmillan, 2011.

Sheppard, Phillis Isabella, Dawn Ottoni Wilhelm, and Ronald J. Allen, eds. *Preaching Prophetic Care: Building Bridges to Justice: Essays in Honor of Dale P. Andrews*. Eugene, OR: Pickwick, 2018.

Smith, Christine M., ed. *Preaching Justice: Ethnic and Cultural Perspectives*. Cleveland, OH: United Church, 1998.

Smith, Mitzi J., and Young-Suk Kim, eds. *Toward Decentering the New Testament: A Reintroduction*. Eugene, OR: Cascade, 2018.

Smith, Ted A. *Weird John Brown: Divine Violence and the Limits of Ethics*. Stanford, CA: Stanford University Press, 2015.

Stevenson, Bryan. *Just Mercy: A Story of Justice and Redemption*. New York: Spiegel & Grau, 2014.

Tanner, Kathryn. *Christianity and the New Spirit of Capitalism*. New Haven, CT: Yale University Press, 2019.

Thomas, Frank A. *How to Preach a Dangerous Sermon*. Nashville: Abingdon, 2018.

Thompson, Lisa L. *Ingenuity: Preaching as an Outsider*. Nashville: Abingdon, 2018.

Tirres, Christopher D. "Embodied Faith in Action: Religious Ritual as Reconstructive Education." In *The Aesthetics and Ethics of Faith: A Dialogue between Liberationist and Pragmatic Thought*, 156–94. New York: Oxford University Press, 2014.

Tisdale, Leonora Tubbs. *Prophetic Preaching: A Pastoral Approach*. Louisville, KY: Westminster John Knox, 2010.

Tonstad, Linn Marie. *Queer Theology: Beyond Apologetics*. Eugene, OR: Cascade, 2018.

Townes, Emilie Maureen. *In a Blaze of Glory: Womanist Spirituality as Social Witness*. Nashville: Abingdon, 1995.

———. *Womanist Ethics and the Cultural Production of Evil*. New York: Palgrave Macmillan, 2006.

Trible, Phyllis. *Texts of Terror: Literary-Feminist Readings of Biblical Narratives*. Philadelphia: Fortress, 1984.

Turman, Eboni Marshall. *Toward a Womanist Ethic of Incarnation: Black Bodies, the Black Church, and the Council of Chalcedon*. New York: Palgrave Macmillan, 2013.

Voelz, Richard William. *Preaching to Teach: Inspire People to Think and Act.* Nashville: Abingdon, 2019.

———. *Youthful Preaching: Strengthening the Relationship between Youth, Adults, and Preaching.* Lloyd John Ogilvie Institute of Preaching Series. Eugene, OR: Cascade, 2016.

Washington, Harriet A. *Medical Apartheid: The Dark History of Experimentation on Black Bodies from Colonial Times to Present.* New York: Doubleday, 2006.

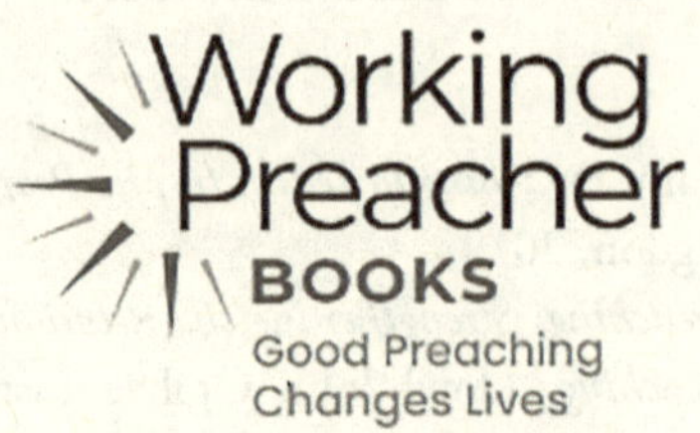

Working Preacher Books is a partnership between Luther Seminary, WorkingPreacher.org, and Fortress Press.

Books in the Series

Preaching from the Old Testament by Walter Brueggemann

Leading with the Sermon: Preaching as Leadership by William H. Willimon

The Gospel People Don't Want to Hear: Preaching Challenging Messages by Lisa Cressman

A Lay Preacher's Guide: How to Craft a Faithful Sermon by Karoline M. Lewis

Preaching Jeremiah: Announcing God's Restorative Passion by Walter Brueggemann

Preaching the Headlines: Possibilities and Pitfalls by Lisa L. Thompson

Honest to God Preaching: Talking Sin, Suffering, and Violence by Brent A. Strawn

Writing for the Ear, Preaching from the Heart by Donna Giver-Johnston

The Peoples' Sermon: Preaching an Embodied Word by Shauna K. Hannan

Real People, Real Faith: Preaching Biblical Characters by Cindy Halvorson

The Visual Preacher: Proclaiming an Embodied Word by Steve Thomason

Divine Laughter: Preaching and the Serious Business of Humor by Karl N. Jacobson and Rolf A. Jacobson

For Every Matter under Heaven: Preaching on Special Occasions by Beverly Zink-Sawyer and Donna Giver-Johnston

Preaching the Gospel of Justice: Good News in Community by Jennifer Ackerman

Digital Homiletics: The Theology and Practice of Online Preaching by Sunggu A. Yang

Midrashic Imagination: Texts and Textures for Pulpit and Pew by Elisabeth R. Jones